INCONVENIENCE STORES

One Year in UK Customer Service

For Pete,

Where it all started.

Best Wishes,

INCONVENIENCE STORES

One Year in UK Customer Service

Mark Bradley

With a Foreword by Adrian Chiles

Ardra Press

First published in 2004 by
Ardra Press
PO Box 78
Cottingham
HU16 4WT
United Kingdom

www.ardrapress.com

ISBN: 0-9548678-1-5

British Library Cataloguing in Publication Data

A CIP record for this book can be obtained from the British Library

Designed and typeset by Julie Martin

Printed and bound by TJ International Ltd, Padstow, Cornwall

Cover design by Ciaron Lee Marlow
www.rockers-going-starwars.co.uk

'We are always getting ready to live, but never living.'

Ralph Waldo Emerson (1834)

To Ana, Luis & Elena

Contents

Foreword

Thanks for buying this book. In fact, I'm not going to thank you. Imagine me just staring at you or, better still, just oblivious to you. It gives me no pleasure at all that you've spent money on this book or that you're bothering to read it. There, you should feel more at home now, because that's customer service as practised in the UK.

My first attempt at writing this foreword consisted of me relating my experiences of poor customer service. Unfortunately, at 75,000 words it was longer than the book itself, so I've had to start again.

You will read this book and feel sure that if you've not actually met some of the characters in it, you've met their twin brothers or sisters. There are a lot of them about and, as Mark Bradley points out, the really significant thing is that they exist in an era where everybody but everybody pays lip service to the importance of customer service. In fact, let's give it a name: customer lip service. There's a lot of that about too.

So what's to be done? My mind goes back to a conference I once moderated for a major bank and credit card supplier. The head of customer service gave a very good speech – albeit, maybe, an extreme example of customer lip service – about how there are three kinds of customer: the evangelists who tell everyone how great the bank is, the neutrals who just roll with it and the terrorists who go round slagging it off.

As it happens, I have had a credit card with that bank for many years. A few months earlier I went to buy a computer with it. The shop assistant looked up at me and said: 'sorry, your card's been refused.' I called the number on the back of the card. 'Sorry, this purchase would take you over your limit.'

'But I've had the card for ten years, I've never exceeded the limit before and I've always [and I realise this is a negative, not a positive, for banks] paid off the bill at the end of the month.'

'Sorry, no.'

'Please.'

'No.'

So now, I explained to the head of this bank's customer service department, I still use the card but just for about a fiver every month which I always pay off. 'That's a nightmare for us,' he said miserably, 'you're a terrorist.' 'Sorry,' I said, unapologetically.

Just as it's an empty cliché for companies to talk about the importance of customer service, it's also sounding a bit thin when people like me stand up and say things like 'just wait till the power of consumers is really harnessed – then we'll show them.' That's not really started to happen yet, and until it does we consumers are partly to blame for the problem.

Adrian Chiles
November 2004

Introduction

A couple of years ago, on the way back home from the nursery, my wife and daughter stopped at the supermarket to pick up one or two things: bread, milk, vegetables and some fruit. Fruit? Well, specifically, grapes. The seedless variety that you bag yourself and then take to the checkout, where they'll be weighed and the price added to your total.

As any parent of a young child will point out to you, in the absence (and possible illegality) of mugging them with chloroform, a couple of grapes can subdue a whingeing infant until you can get her into the car and back home for a good telling-off (even though it seems that these days most people stay at the supermarket to hit their kids). Anyway, and not for the first time, our daughter saw the opportunity to nibble and was helping herself to a grape as my wife approached the checkout.

'Excuse me, Madam,' interjected the cashier, while processing another customer's shopping, 'that's an unweighed bag of grapes. What you're actually doing is shoplifting.'

When my wife recounted this story to me later, she laughed off the allegation. I, on the other hand, didn't. Retail self-destruction was never more evident.

And what makes me more peeved is the fact that, when I get home and switch on the TV, the most reliable reflector of service culture (and dictator thereof occasionally), I get hour upon hour of garden makeovers, celebrity chefs, style gurus and home makeovers. All of these elements have drained into service culture, like so much dishwater. But the concept of service – good old customer service, the heart of all successful enterprises – remains curiously untapped.

Essential image consultants introduce that latest shirt and skirt combo, lifting you from dowdy to pouting in a few magical moments, and tousle-haired landscape designers build the Guggenheim in your back garden. But they soon exit your conscience, leaving nothing more substantial than sickly superficiality, a veneer as plainly thin and translucent as a discarded toenail. Customer service, however, only interests the media in respect of 'goods' and/or 'products' like when it can expose malpractice, catch a dodgy builder in the act or uncover a huge bootlegging operation.

For me, it's suffered a profile lower than a daschund's genitals.

The bright-eyed 9-year-old tells his parents, 'I want to get into law,' and they gleam back at him, pride washing through their body like a champagne enema. Or he tells them, 'I want to get into medicine,' and they imagine future visits to numerous simpering grandchildren in glorious Cotswold retreats. However, the one child who tells his parents, 'I want to get into customer service,' inevitably generates an image of a fast food operative – 'do you want fries with that?'

I believed that good service was the cumulative output of emotionally engaged employees attending to a higher purpose, conducive surroundings, good, reliable products and the feeling of 'value'.

I believed that it was about people who care, caring about people who were expecting indifference or inflexibility. It's about organisations who value their employees, who have an interest in their lives beyond work, who develop them and who let them have their say. It's that fantastic recovery, the results of such an environment, when things were going wrong. It's the unexpected extra that oxygenates the everyday transaction.

And yet, despite the millions of pounds invested into 'brand management', 'product development' and the like, it's service that differentiates. The same service that, I feared, lacked investment, training and commitment in the majority of organisations today.

But 'Customer Service' investment has spiralled into the 'must do' category, starting with business process re-engineering in the early nineties through change programmes, customer focus, customer centricity to the latest in a long line of cool monikers: customer experience management.

There are several obvious pieces of learning for the interested organisation and accountants can detail the millions of pounds invested in bringing the theories into life. Charter Mark engages the Public Sector and year after year the number of celebratory customer service awards and conferences must reflect the improvement in frontline service.

Job offers now carry the mandatory 'must have excellent customer service skills' and every retail interview contains a 'what if ...' service scenario for the new recruit to address.

But has any of this made a difference? Has any of this effort brought a reward for the UK shopper?

A senior manager at a previous employer with over 800 retail branches once said that, after all of the flurry of investment in change and agility in the mid-nineties, the experience of visiting one of his branches had stubbornly refused to reveal the slightest difference or improvement to the experience. Cut forward ten years and, for most of us I suspect, the decoration may have changed, but the desolation remains the same.

Dr Frankenstein had his dreams, but created a monster. Poor service performance generates frustrated customers, whose growing disenchantment in turn makes them more likely to turn on employees. This, in turn, erodes any positive attitude they may have brought into the organisation or had fostered by an inspirational manager.

So, let's return to my wife's unfortunate supermarket visit and the service that was lacking that day. Not that stealing grapes should be scratched from the CPS's list of crimes, of course.

Even if my wife was guilty of unintentionally removing

items without paying, isn't it good practice to turn a blind eye to something which makes kids behave, which in turn makes employees and customers happier and more relaxed, which in turn makes the latter more likely to spend more time in your store, which in turn leads them to spend more money in your store, which in turn leads you to make the sort of profits you got into business for in the first place?

Get your calculators out, kids. How much is a grape worth to the supermarket? How does it compare to the total profit they make from a regular shopper, say, over the six years they live in the neighbourhood?

The fact that the UK's leading supermarkets, Asda (Britain's favourite supermarket 2004) and Tesco (Britain's favourite business 2003), routinely encourage their employees to make the link between the customer's lifetime value to the business and the quality of service provided, appears to offer a business case for not getting too hung up on the vine.

The cost of taking time to service their needs and create a comfortable environment in which to make their purchases appears to make financial sense. Given that £12 of every £100 spent in the UK ends up in a Tesco till (according to the press in December 2003), I'm tempted to concede that it does.

This rival, who is, after all, selling the same range of products in the same traditional supermarket way appears, in the eyes of most city commentators, to be lagging far behind.

But when I wrote in to complain about my wife's treatment, they conceded that the cashier had selected an unfortunate combination of words, but gave no ground on the justification for the comment (other than enclosing a £10 voucher, which still had a small yellow post-it attached with the message 'Give him a £10 voucher').

So does my wife's experience offer an insight into where one of their greatest opportunities may lie? Or is this, on my part, just sour grapes?

Back at the start of 2003 I set off on a voyage of discovery.

Armed with a notebook and a long list of acquaintances primed to contact me with their own stories, I began my pioneering odyssey.

My experiences are grouped together in the months in which they occurred. While most of them relate to 2003, many more have occurred since putting my thoughts to paper in 2004. However, they do share one important component – absolute accuracy. There is no exaggeration, no hyperbole to engage the anger of the reader or expose the joy of a great service experience. There is, I admit, a Bryson-esque attempt at livening up the travelogue with some rich description, but I've resisted every urge to commit imagined events to paper.

Sometimes – and, thinking back, most times – the absence of any rich feedback reflects the dourness of the experience and the lack of meaningful notes on my part. Other times, the joy or disappointment influences the mind's eye and the description may be more colourful than it was, but these are the perceptions that are going to be shared by every customer… so there!

So what have I found? How does UK retail perform? Who's great to do business with? Who's the best at sorting out problems? Who couldn't give a proverbial?

I set out with two intended beneficiaries. Firstly, we band of customers, we happy few (albeit outnumbered by a huge group of unhappy ones). If we pooled our individual influence and started to vote with our feet, maybe things would change. Are we to blame for accepting and, therefore, colluding with poor standards of service? Is our behaviour so unbecoming that we've driven frontline employees to a state of nervous aggression? Should we, as my good friend John once did, stand in the centre of a shop and proclaim how poor its service is, encouraging everyone to go elsewhere? Shall we set up Internet communities to shake up UK retail?

Secondly, I want to help the people in these organisations themselves. If, as someone once cleverly put it, 'companies are perfectly designed to achieve their results,' could my odyssey inform organisational design?

Could we create a compelling business case for change that would stir the most unconscious financial director or actuary? Could we trace an outline of an uncompromisingly human business philosophy that delivers time and time again for all stakeholders, be they employees, customers, employers or the community?

Could taking the customer perspective generate learning for organisations? Might these examples encourage some reflection and adoption of new ideas? Could my intentionally constructive criticism stir a chicken shack of directors into some positive activity?

Is this whole endeavour going to be hamstrung by the realisation that we customers, employees and employers are all us! We may adopt the different roles, but they all reflect the riotous complexities of the human psyche.

Ultimately, I wanted to push the concept of great service out into the limelight. If garden makeovers, soapumentaries on Mallorcan hairdressers and selling your house can become part of popular culture so quickly, isn't service deserving of the same accolade? I want to drag customer service into popular culture now.

So, without wishing to spoil the surprise for the casual reader, the experience has not been a continuous procession of ecstatic moments of joy. There have been a few rays of light through the clouds, but not nearly enough to lift the gloom from this unhappy shopper.

November 2004

1

January

'I don't know how we get away with charging £1.90 each for these muffins. As you've already bought a load of sandwiches from us, I'm only going to charge you a pound each for them. Is that OK?'

Proprietor of upmarket sandwich bar
in Lincolnshire Shopping Mall.

From my limited knowledge of Greek mythology I gather that an odyssey is the story of a journey – a quest, if you like. I imagine Jason and his Argonauts battling Ray Harryhausen's scary plasticine figures in their search for the Golden Fleece and hiding behind columns, trying to avoid meeting the eyes of the Gorgon for fear of being petrified. I see the huge Achilles figure toppling over on the beach as the myriads of Argonauts dislodge the plug from his heel. I see Harry Hamlin from *Clash of the Titans* getting creative with his reflective shield as he parts Medusa's head from her scaly body.

Perseus, Jason and their rapidly reducing number of cohorts would be welcome to join me in my quest for good service in the UK, but I doubt they'd have the resilience, valour or determination to emerge triumphant. Especially now that the sales have just commenced, where hand-to-hand combat over the crockery at Selfridges makes the opening half an hour of *Saving Private Ryan* look like an episode of *Teletubbies*.

Someone I know at Old Trafford summarised the customer service challenge at Manchester United as 'getting 67,000 people into a venue and sat down in less than 45 minutes'. Yep, you don't have time to engage every one in three with a free latte and a chat about the weather and their future pur-chasing requirements. It's all about getting to the front of the queue and getting your hands on that frosted champagne glass set at Next. Quite frankly, you'd buy those Next jeans at that price, even if the staff smelt of alcohol and spent the whole time picking their noses. As I write, I hear that over 100,000 cars have turned up at the Trafford Centre on Boxing Day 2003 to explore a mall designed to park 10,000 cars.

But we tag on to the hordes with no greater hope than to emerge unscathed into the Trafford evening, armed with our booty. Such are the great majority of interactions in our everyday lives: necessary purchases, like petrol or cash with-drawals or visits to the Post Office. We have limited expecta-tions: quick reliable service and exit stage left.

I suspect this is not going to provide a controlled environ-ment for fair mystery shopping. In fact, you'll need so much fortitude, it'll have to be fivetitude.

Either way, it's life, it happens. It helps stores clear out old stock for the arrival of the new. It drives footfall and some-times leads to other purchases, not from main sale stock. But what intrigues me is that, when it comes to the push (a par-ticularly appropriate metaphor for January shopping), does the popularity of the January Sales mean that retail business success is just about a good price?

A pretty silly question, because if it did, we'd have sales all the year round. Hang on a minute, we do! Or at least we have a whole lot more than we used to have. There's always a sale rail in Gap. There's even a sale section of my favourite foot-ball team's website. In fact, things have been so bad lately that you could pick up a central midfielder for a few quid.

Anyone worth his lo-salt will tell you that being cheapest isn't always the best. **www.cdwow.co.uk** is a fantastically cheap place to get CDs. As I write this, most items in stock are £8.99 and post and packing comes free. However, in my experience, they only stock chart or recent-chart titles, so those of us looking for the more obscure item are likely to find **www.amazon.co.uk** or **www.hmv.co.uk** a better option.

These propositions are sound (although the former is currently being besieged by accusations from its competitors that its mass buying of Asian-produced CDs is unfair) and apparently successful. The 'cheapest is best' argument is already developing a tickly cough.

I know that many retail organisations that routinely collect feedback from their customers have discovered a direct correlation between enthusiastic, responsive and empathetic employees and persistency – the intention to recommend the organisation and buy more from it.

One building society calculates that investing in the look and feel of the branch office, uniforms and shiny new logos has no impact whatsoever on the customer's intention to remain loyal or commit more.

It's also proven that in times of relative economic stability, interest rates are of far less concern to branch-visiting customers than the quality of the welcome and the readiness to help they observe.

But for now, as we emerge scathed from Next, let's continue our merry journey.

This chapter is entitled 'January' and the intention was to begin this odyssey in the first month of the year, to coincide with the traditional start of the sales. However, as they now begin in late December, so do I.

It came to pass that a combination of dark forces caused our bathroom taps to malfunction. This required a trip to the hardware store, so early on 28 December we set off to our nearest DIY & hardware store in West Yorkshire.

Having found the taps we wanted and discovered that this would involve using their 'collect and serve' service, we picked up one of the vouchers with the product detail on (there were several remaining) and cheerfully made our way to the deserted 'collect and serve' counter to receive our items.

For me, this was an immediate disappointment, my reason being that this specific establishment has a particularly enlightened approach to recruitment which, among other things, encourages the more mature conscript, who usually has more than a passing acquaintance with the concept of customer care. On this occasion, however, they were either delayed by the admittedly testing distance from one end of the store to the other, or had not yet actually been recruited.

After a while an assistant appeared, greeted us and took the voucher away. Unfortunately, he couldn't find the item we wanted. Not 'out of stock' or else there wouldn't have been any vouchers, one imagined. He just couldn't find it. To be fair to him, he asked a colleague, who told him where to look but wouldn't go with him. More on personal ownership later (if I can be bothered).

A second trip to the cupboard proved as fruitless as an orange tree in Oldham and we left disappointed with yours truly whining to my kids about the lack of service.

In spite of my protestations, we arrived at a sister store some 20 minutes later. This time the taps were on show, but there were no vouchers. A nice turnaround, like waiting 15 years for your baby to grow up so you can go out, get inebriated, come home and be sick on him. Unimpressed, but undeterred, we looked for assistance. The store wasn't busy, but there was no one around, so we waited expectantly for the tumbleweed to drift past us.

There was one guy, whizzing about on an industrial floor cleaner, but he was wearing that 'don't you dare involve me' face and appeared to regard dramatic acceleration as the best way to avoid being pinned down by a customer.

While my wife searched in vain for assistance, I returned to the 'collect and serve' counter and waited patiently. Godot finally came, in the person of a cashier who had used the PA to call for assistance at 'collect and serve', but who had given up hope of any response and had come across herself.

As my kids settled in for a long stay, our taps were finally found. So to summarise, plenty of vouchers but no taps in store one and plenty of taps but no vouchers in store two.

And £67 for my trouble.

And that's the part that hurts, as I feel helpless. We need the taps (and they might get fitted one day) and it pains me to reward the dreadful service with my money. But I won't be buying taps there again, if I can help it!

In addition to a wide range of products and generally good prices, this company probably has the best of intentions. They also have good distribution around the UK. But there doesn't seem to be a process in place to prevent experiences such as ours from re-occurring and the overall impression is that the opportunity to build on their good reputation is either not seen or not understood, or, perhaps more accurately, represents an unnecessary and unwelcome investment in more people.

What would be a simple first step would be for people there to walk round the store as a 'customer'. It's only then that some of the service obstacles reveal themselves. I can see the response now: if I abandon my post to go in the customer's shoes for a while, then when I need something from me, I won't be there, thus exacerbating the problem. Fair point. But how many UK organisations actually care sufficiently to spend time understanding what their customers actually encounter when they step into your world?

Interestingly, visiting the place for some compost in early 2004, I come across a meeting of employees in the middle of the garden department. The manager is explaining business performance and covering off points of administration. I wonder if he's covered off 'taps' yet.

Sunday 29 December, friends of mine travelling to see Newcastle United play Blackburn, arrive in town early so their son can get into the record store to exchange his vouchers for a 'Medal of Honour' PlayStation® game. For security reasons, there are dozens of empty copies on the shelf (perhaps an attempt to emulate the marvellous 'collect and serve' approach), so he picks up a copy and takes it to the checkout desk. 'Sorry. Sold out,' he is told. Happy New Year!

Upon returning home to Shropshire the family discover a fault with their heating system. A pity, since this has turned out to be the coldest period of the year, and as they have only recently moved into a new house this is disappointing, but perhaps forgivable. Until, that is, they attempted to contact the builder.

To summarise, he contacts the Customer Assistance line at 2pm on 30 December. He's told that the systems are down but someone will ring back. They don't. At 9pm, without hot water and with only a gas fire to keep himself, his wife and three children warm, he rings the 24/7 hotline again only to be told that it's closed until 5 January. Or perhaps 24/7 means only 7 out of 24 calls ever get answered.

His next step is to email the company explaining his anger and frustration at the quality of service, instructing them that if he doesn't get a satisfactory response he will contact a service engineer himself and send the builder the bill.

Strangely enough, this prompts a response. Better late than never. But isn't it strange that companies only stir themselves from their torpor either when faced with newspaper or television exposure or when it dawns on them that they're going to have to pay out a larger sum of money than they'd anticipated?

So, why is it permissible for a builder to sell you a house, one assumes at a decent profit in these house price inflation times, and yet not fulfil the most basic after-sales service promise? Is it because they know you can't take the house back and swap it for a new one? Or is it because they think that people will just accept poor service, since this is what they're used to receiving in every other walk of life? What I do know is that this particular customer in Shropshire would need persuading to buy from this company again, even if the location was right.

Now most people buy new houses on the basis of the house design and its location – not because the builder has a cool brand name. This contrasts greatly with the experience of some Virgin customers, who felt unease at the transfer of ownership of the One Account to Royal Bank of Scotland, as the Virgin name might be departing their cash cards and chequebooks.

It's the same account after all. And, as far as I know, the

same team in Norwich that administer it. But somehow the knowledge that a bank (and, so it seems, a pretty good one) is pulling the strings seems less appealing.

Any company under the Virgin moniker does enjoy warmth from the public (we'll deal with Virgin Trains later). The Virgin 'promise' appears to have a lot to do with taking the customer's side. It appears to be based on differentiated service.

Well you've probably guessed it, but I do think that service is the main differentiator (as well as the way they design their organisations – which we'll come to later). I could argue that having pretty yellow and red visa cards might be what's lighting people's wicks, but I'll reserve that revelation for another time. The perception that you matter as a customer is the warm, unexpected spark that ignites your passion. I promise not to extend this fire-related euphemism any further.

So, let's consider lesson one in my chronological inspection of UK service: personal ownership.

Today, 17 January, my wife, children and I take our regular Saturday walk around our local town. Before I hear from West Yorkshire-based lawyers, let me state without hesitation that our small Pennine town boasts some fine establishments (some of which I'll come to later), but it also has the usual share of national chains, with the attendant lack of consistency that I have come to love – well, love in the reassuring consistency meaning of the word.

'Let's buy a lottery ticket!' suggests my wife, as we pass a national newsagent / book retailer / stationery dispenser (hey, maybe they're just doing too much), displaying a confidence in fortune that had long deserted this miserable shopper. 'You never know!'

In order to achieve this objective without starting world war III, my kids are asked to select three numbers each as they stand outside the store. In response, they refuse steadfastly to budge from choosing 6 numbers between 20 and 30.

At last my son and I enter and notice that the lottery ticket machine has been recently re-sited from the calmer 'book and writing implements' side of the store to the frenetic 'newspaper-buying' centre. There are two cashiers, one either side of the machine. We choose the smaller queue (five people) and wait.

When I finally push my son's numbers across the till, we are told, 'we only do the lottery from the other side'. Happy New Year to you too, you miserable git.

How much would it cost to say, 'Thank you sir, here's your ticket. But just to save you time in future, we usually only serve lottery tickets from the other side.'

Hey, you know I might think, 'that's a good idea: at least they're trying out something new to see if they can manage the flow of people a little better. You've got to take your hat off to them, too: they forgave us and served us anyway.'

But what I actually believe, as we begin what becomes a 12-person queue (that featured prominently a number of people for whom the weekly purchase of the entire neighbourhood's lottery tickets was akin to a raging orgasm), is sadly not printable, even in as common a publication as this one.

If I were to carry out a survey of UK organisations and were to ask them where customer service ranked in order of priority, they'd all rank it at number one (or number two in the odd case). So how come it doesn't happen in practice? What a load of rankers.

This particular store is usually a reliable place to go. Just last week, one of the floor-walking employees noticed that I was carrying a couple of books and took the time to let me know that if I took a third it would come free of charge as part of a 'three for two' offer. I was impressed. I thanked her. She looked happy. I told a couple of people with me what had happened. They were impressed – and while I don't recall them sprinting from the store to broadcast the information on CB radio, as a subject for discussion it lingered longer than a post-asparagus visit to the toilet and was equally invigorating.

So how come the new recruit hasn't been told about 'ownership' and 'initiative'? But I think I'll give them a second chance. Inconsistent, but apparently caring enough to set into motion some processes designed to reciprocate our patronage.

So the Monday comes and I take the train south. Again, this is usually a reliable affair. A trip of less than two hours for £132 standard return. Where else could you be shaken around so quickly for such amounts (other than a sauna I know, or rather, that I have been told about)?

The train company appear to pride themselves on the service levels they provide, which is probably quite a risk given the state of the infrastructure one imagines they send their trains along each day. But my experience has, by and large, been very good. In fact, I sense that they have anticipated that travellers in the UK are so 'down' on the railways generally, that conflict management and service recovery skills probably form the main part of an induction process.

On this occasion, it was one of those big long ones (excuse the technical term) with so many carriages that the train doesn't need to move to get you from A to B.

My records show it was the 0620 train and, as you might reasonably imagine, my fellow travellers fancied a bacon and tomato toasted sandwich.

As we arrived in the expansive buffet lounge we began to be enveloped by the suffocating gloom only truly appreciated by the UK citizen – the slow queue. Like a slow puncture, it takes you ages to find out why there's a problem, until you immerse the subject in water. While two business colleagues and myself calculated how we would achieve this without drawing the attention of the guard, someone noticed that it was the fact that the bacon was being cooked to order.

Now, like the next man (who was, by this time, crying with hunger), I like my food fresh. However, I am prepared to accept that the rail traveller might concede a little 'fast food' would be appropriate in such circumstances.

But in this case it seemed that the free-range pig, who was making the ultimate commitment, had been trotted out this morning for some exercise before being rendered unconscious with a piece of track. We imagined the unfortunate pig had begun the curing process and our sandwiches would be ready by the next millennium.

However, the sandwiches slowly began to arrive. It was at this point that two foreign businessmen behind me finally put in their order. 'A continental breakfast, please, and an all-day breakfast too?' they tentatively asked, obviously having some experience of UK service. A request so tentative, you suspected they'd been here before.

Neither item was available, leading us to concur that, in some strange experiment, these folk had abandoned the usual concepts of the conventional eating schedule and would be about to serve up a curry.

At this point they presented a £50 note for payment. Unsurprisingly, there was insufficient change to accept that, so eventually a credit card was used. On the way back as I made several further visits to the buffet bar I noticed that on each occasion the values of the notes considered too big to change were dropping dramatically. Later that day, on the way back, a tenner was greeted with the same disdain met by its wealthier cousin the same morning.

This all leads one to surmise that operational efficiency may be somewhat lacking and that it requires addressing as urgently as the leaf-strewn tracks upon which we glided, or glid, or glud, for that matter.

The personal touch is always present on these rail journeys and while admitting the difficulties of recreating quality dining facilities on the move, there is room for improvement. But my rail experiences have thrown up some positive experiences, a few of which I list in later chapters.

Admittedly my January experiences are a varied lot – but January's an interesting time. People have generally exhaust-ed not only their savings, but also most of their credit cards and, by the middle of the month, their tempers too. As a con-sequence, as we, the great unwashed, watch *Takeshi's Castle*, we are faced with a barrage of credit offers to soften us up in between Craig Charles's endless repetition of the 'ring penetration' joke.

However, what interests me this time is an observation made by my beloved. She pointed out that a car credit advert had abandoned the overt promise of support in favour of opting for the conditional. What was once, 'Can I get a decent interest rate? Yes, you can!' has been surreptitiously replaced with, 'could I get a decent interest rate? Yes, you could.' The latter perhaps implies, 'no, you can't'. 'Unless you go somewhere else,' one assumes.

Which brings me to the proliferation of service promises made in the UK. A recent research study found that larger organisations are regular offenders, making the most assurances about service but then failing to deliver.

However, service promises and standards continue to occupy the minds of UK organisations. Many's the call I've had enquiring after 'a decent list of service standards' as if it were an 'off the shelf' option. In many cases, such standards are seen as part of good customer service. That may be the case (especially when they are actually fulfilled in front of the customer), but in general terms, they are never supported by sanctions.

A few years ago the UK Passport Office inherited the moniker 'The Piss Poor Office' from my family when we had to wait an age for our passport. The Passport Office has actually been awarded a Government Charter Mark, which necessitates, among other things, a list of service standards. And yet when things go wrong and these standards are not met, what is the sanction? Correct. There isn't one. It brings to mind the old Robin Williams line about the unarmed British policeman chasing a thief: 'Stop, thief, or … I'll shout "stop, thief" again.'

Yes, my friend, you have learned that a service promise, consistently and regularly fulfilled, is about as rare as a TV ad without either a Tom Baker, Gina McKee or Juliet Stevenson voice-over.

Service promises do actually proliferate in the US and

are held up by many customer service reporters as being broadly effective. However, most of our stateside cousins appear to find service just as frustrating over there as it is here. Service promises can be as painful as unrequited love. You give so much: your time and commitment, devotion and money. You expect so much and receive a cold shoulder.

Another frustrating element of service promises, which we will return to again and again, is the fact that most customers, in my experience, want the phone answered relatively promptly by someone prepared to be courteous, to listen and to have the flexibility to meet any range of requests. Whether the phone is answered in five or fifteen rings is less important.

When I'm holding and I hear the recorded message 'your call is important to us. Please hold and an operator will be with you soon.' I think, 'no it isn't. If it were, you would have enough operators to answer the phone.'

When I happen upon MBNA, the message says, and I paraphrase, 'because we take as much time as each customer needs, there may be a small delay before we get to you.' That's better. At least I am soothed by a customer-focused explanation for the delay.

Personal ownership, on the other hand, a function of the human characteristics of the person with whom you are dealing, is akin to the joyful reunion of Tim and Dawn at the end of *The Office Christmas Special.* Hoped for but not expected, and richly rewarding.

Rewarding not only for you, the previously unhappy shopper, but also for your customer service assistant, who radiates with the satisfaction of having done a great job. You'll go there again. You'll tell someone about it. They'll beam for a few more moments and might repeat the experience for the next customer.

Or you could be me. It's January and I have to give a presentation at a hotel in Kettering. I arrive at a deserted hotel armed with a laptop, from which I need to make a copy of a diskette. I enter the bar area. It's mid afternoon. Not busy.

'Can I have a cup of tea, please?'

'Yes, sir.'

'Have you got any crisps? I'm a bit peckish.'

'No. But there are some nibbles on the bar and your tea comes with biscuits.'

'OK then. Have you somewhere here where I can plug my laptop in? My battery's playing up and I need to copy a diskette.'

'No. It isn't allowed.'

While I wondered what was illegal about copying diskettes, I had, yet again, encountered our friend Mr Total Lack of Ownership. First visit to this hotel – and quite frankly, probably the last. Am I being cruel? Maybe so. But all I wanted was somewhere to plug my laptop in.

There's also the demeanour of the individual. This is something that will define the year ahead for me. A disjointed conversation, a lack of genuine interest, the face the result of many years' research into developing the perfect expression for conveying disinterest. The semantics of the body language communicate so much awkwardness, so much indifference; this is not the language of love.

On the way out later I noticed the business section of the hotel, apparently set up to deal with such emergencies. It was never pointed out to me that it even existed. I would have happily exchanged a few pounds for the service, but the glum woman behind the bar wasn't having any.

Does this employee know that hotels need to pay money to keep people in work in quiet bars in mid-week January afternoons? Wouldn't a briefing be welcome? Obviously not.

But I did set off with the intention of helping UK organisations. So, what are organisations doing to address this, assuming (and this is a dangerous one) that they see the benefits?

Quite frankly, very little. Or so it would seem. Or let me put it this way: several organisations appear to have figured it out, leading to their acceleration in the Premier League of service, leaving others trailing in their wake.

I promise you this book will not be full of 'easy guides' and 'top tips', but ownership is so lacking everywhere I go, that I can't resist. So here's my top ten of ways to improve ownership:

1 Be open and honest with your people about the prevailing business context. Don't just take them away to the NEC once a year to shout at them (albeit with a troupe of actors and some jazzy graphics). Build a discussion into the weekly schedule. In that way, especially for the larger organisations, you can reproduce the environment of the small, independent retailer, whose employees are often close relatives and who know that their livelihood hinges on the quality of every interaction with the public.

2 Reward people for doing things that show they've understood the business context and are applying it practically on a day-to-day basis. For example, bending or ignoring a convention or rule that, in the specific circumstances, benefits neither your employee nor the customer.

3 Explore, with your employees, ways to reward and/or recognise these examples. A journalist friend of mine is sceptical about the potential of 'tree-hugging' activities in his industry – and I have to agree – and yet Henry Stewart, founder of Happy Computers (**www.happy.co.uk**), undeniably one of the UK's great success stories of the past decade (and once a journalist, as if that should somehow confer upon him a higher degree of scepticism than the rest of us), was driven to success by the belief that 'people work better when they feel good about themselves'. Make sure your floorwalkers 'thank' people when they see good practice. Actually, for many of you reading this, just getting your people to floorwalk would be a start!

4 Ask your people what information they need to be able to do a good job. As someone once famously said, 'When I employ someone's hands, their brain comes free!'

5 Give your people the time and space to practise personal ownership by removing 'over management' and agreeing to reduce the number of priorities they have. A recent survey of a wholesaler's branch employees produced the

comment: 'with every extra sales report, time and motion study and data return, you reduce our time with the customer.'

6 Get your own management to spend a week with frontline colleagues and see how they apply personal ownership. It helps them understand the obstacles to service.

7 Be decisive about discouraging bad practice. If there are people in your business who, in spite of your expressed support (let's say you're doing all of the above) do not want to 'play ball', then put them in the 'sin bin' or, to stretch the American Sports analogy beyond its reasonable limit, 'introduce them to The Fridge'. Most employees appear to be dismissed for not producing sales. Very few for not producing service. And what leads to sales? Thank you, children. Please take an apple.

8 Figure problems out with your people. Sit down with them and explore some of the daily scenarios with them. If a bank branch is packed to the Pat Rafters every lunchtime and you can't afford extra resources, what impact does your ignoring the problem have on your frontline people? Hey, even if your people are seen to be making an effort in such circumstances by apologising, putting every available pair of hands on a till or floorwalking to explain the use of the ATM, it's better than nothing and, funnily enough, it does mitigate against customer attrition.

9 Train your people properly. Yer average 'sales process' has gems in it like 'greeting and welcome', 'identify needs', 'overcome objectives' and 'gain commitment' – all designed to be hastily imposed on the unwitting customer rather than designed to create a conducive environment to promote your services. Where does 'personal ownership' come into this? Well, about as welcome as the next series of *Pop Idol*, since you ask.

10 Start to take performance management seriously. Get your managers consistently to observe, give feedback, discuss problems openly and coach – day-in, day-out, not

just every quarter because HR tells them to. Get them to focus on 'personal ownership' for a while. Get your senior people to drop by and find out what's going on. Get them to ask, 'what specifically have you done to help improve levels of personal ownership?' If they can't answer, introduce them to your friends, the dogs: their favourite food is faces.[1]

But this doesn't appear to happen. Why not? There's not enough time. We're too busy. We've so much on at the moment. Tell you what: we customers will go somewhere else, so you have time to do this stuff.

Compare and contrast, please. A friend visits Iceland's online shopping service and makes her choice. What arrives is not what she ordered, so she telephones. The woman who had picked her consignment told her: 'I spotted that you could have had more for the money, by taking advantage of one or two new offers, so I took the liberty of making the changes for you. Was that all right?'

Of course it was all right.

Another friend discovers that the apparently fresh chicken she has just bought at Asda either has a disturbing body odour problem or is, in fact, going off dramatically. Upon returning the chicken to the store she receives not only a new and extremely fragrant chicken, but also has the original cost refunded. We'll come to how this excellent approach to service recovery has joined my burgeoning list of missed UK business opportunities later.

And there are some, frankly, silly ones too. Forgive me if the following has become apocryphal but it illustrates my point.

Several Christmases ago, one of our best-known supermarkets was experiencing a problem. Their recently launched 'Turkey Order' system had run smoothly all the way through Christmas Eve until the very last turkey accompanied its owner home. At this point, as the team

---

[1] Thank you to Johnny Bravo, in whose cartoon series this wonderful threat originally appeared

congratulated itself for a sound performance, a little old lady began her slow walk towards them. 'I've come to pick up my turkey,' she announced to general dismay.

Why General Dismay was present is indeed a good question. But even if he had been there, with a crack troop of logistics experts, he couldn't have summoned a turkey from nothing.

Having exhausted all available routes (ignoring the obvious one of calling the local butcher: 'Hi. We're the big powerful supermarket trying to put you out of business. Can you lend us a turkey, please?'), they tried to contact their local suppliers. While this was going on, one of the team, for reasons that are known only to him, was thinking about Lee Majors – the bionic man. After a short pause, he announced, 'We can re-build it,' and immediately set about amassing a curious hybrid of turkey legs, chicken breasts, pork loin and various appendages whose cumulative affect was to suggest a well-lived-in turkey.

To cut a long story short, the little old gal left with the promise of a turkey delivery by Christmas morn, as well as the bionic Bird, dressed to the nines with a seasonal garnish, for her trouble.

But such imagination is rare in this country. Elsewhere however, a different story emerges.

On a trip to the US a couple of years ago I happened to drop into Borders in Chicago. Having made my purchases and arrived at the cash desk I was warmly greeted. When my answer betrayed my status as a tourist, the youngster in front of me asked what I was doing in town. 'I'm making a presentation on customer service at a conference,' I told him. 'So, I guess you could say you're a sort of customer service teacher?' he offered. 'I suppose you could.'

'Well,' he continued, his face opening up into a beaming smile, 'it's teachers' week here in Borders, so we can give you a 30% discount off all your purchases today.'

Would that it were ever customers' week in this country during this long cold month.

2

February

'Would you like to win £7,000?'
'No.'

Interaction between sales rep and customer overheard
outside Beattie's department store in Huddersfield,
West Yorkshire (February 2003).

Speaking of Americans, my signature anecdote involves a compatriot of our friend in Chicago. A respected Harvard lecturer on culture change and customer focus, he was in a Pennine town to work with a large building society which was based there.

After a particularly testing session with a group of managers he decided to take a visit to the town centre to get a coffee.

This being 1995 and the coffee house explosion still some five years away in this isolated outpost, he should have known better than to ask for a cappuccino in a local and, at the time, the principal Coffee House. 'You'll have to go to Leeds if you want one of those,' came the retort in a flat, tar-soaked West Yorkshire growl.

And yet the continental love of coffee has finally enveloped us here in the UK. Every other high street establishment is one of the big national chains or one of a myriad of small independent coffee bars.

Notably, many of these coffee bars follow the American model, in that they want to provide a relaxing area, conducive to replenishing energy, with an array of quality products, served by caring, attentive and knowledgeable staff. Interestingly, UK versions appear to be able to do all of this (apart from the six elements described above). Service as flat as a skinny latte.

Interestingly, I identified several of these establishments as fitting the profile required for my odyssey. And I found this to be interestingly interesting.

Picture the scene. Synchronise watches. 0645 hours, M6, southbound. Approaching the motorway services station. Blood sugar level worryingly low. BBC Radio 5's Nicky Campbell worryingly wry. Coffee required. Coffee shop sign noted. Your tongue limbers up for a taste sensation.

The coffee shop doesn't open until 0700 at these services (and just about everywhere else, as a matter of fact). And yet, as the pressure of work increases and the conventional working day extends from early morning to late evening, isn't it reassuring to see organisations blithely ignoring these socio-demographic changes and failing to respond to the need?

Just in case my need for caffeine had bordered on the hysterical, the coffee section had been surrounded by a circle of chairs, to resist attempts by customers to storm their refrigerated window.

Never mind. Any visit to a service station involves a visit to the gentlemen's washroom (assuming you're a male). By way of consolation, perhaps. But have you noticed the proliferation of push buttons, as you leave, requesting that you rate the experience, so that they can improve in future?

Have a closer look (remembering which experience they want you to rate). Feedback on offers written on the walls of service station cubicles is not generally sought – although, one imagines, it's infinitely more intriguing.

There's an example set of results showing a dramatic increase in the levels of satisfaction over a six-month period. They must be improving, you tell yourself, until you discover that these results are 'example' results. There was a big clue in the words 'example results' but I'm not at my sharpest at such early hours. Perhaps they're just going through the motions. Ouch. Forgive that. I understand this has since been changed, but it amused me at the time. But I'd be more interested in the actual figures. I also guess that service station managers would be more interested in actual performance than imagined, however motivating it is to know that your customers are pooing in increasing comfort as the year rolls by.

This brings us to my theme for February – being open to feedback. What do I mean by this? Well, let's assume you complain to the DIY store because they never seem to have your taps in stock. Those of us who haven't had every last drop of enthusiasm squeezed from us, expect little more than an acknowledgement and an apology (and we're often lucky to get the latter). What I want to know is: who are the companies that take our feedback seriously and do something about it?

From my travels, they are not legion. In fact, I'm beginning to think they're not even plural. And yet, what better way of improving service and impressing people with your customer focus, than through taking our feedback on board and having a process to analyse it and turn it into progress.

At this point, I'm in a large toy retail store, armed with money from my son's savings account (a situation being repeated more and more often throughout the year – mostly without his knowledge – and without him benefiting either). Having identified our purchase, we approach the till.

The cashier, making a special effort to look particularly uninterested, asks me if I have the reward card. My response is, as I recall, 'I'd prefer it if it was like the Tesco reward card, so I could save points and buy anything I wanted, rather than receiving discount vouchers through the post that only relate to specific purchases.'

I watch her complete indifference and feebly conclude my explanation with a barely audible, 'so, er, that's why I don't carry it.'

Having offered what I considered to be constructive feedback, you might expect the opportunity to be leapt upon.

It isn't even given a cursory glance from behind a figurative distant bush. In fact, to make the point that my feedback isn't welcome, the cashier begins to serve the next customer.

Thus began our new family game – full of fun and laughs – entitled 'Let's give the toy store some constructive feedback'. I recall Bill Hicks announcing his retirement from stand-up comedy to front a CBS TV special entitled *Let's Hunt and Kill Billy Ray Cyrus*. I recall him getting quite vocal in his derision for the pony-tailed lothario. Such is my current frustration with the toy store.

On a second occasion, with my kids giggling, I try the same approach. A genuine offer of constructive feedback designed to benefit both customers and the business is given. I hope I'm around to give it when 'both' customers are all they have left.

So we've found one organisation that shows results that don't relate to actual feedback and another to whom feedback is clearly akin to the 'lurgy' and is something that should be resisted at all costs.

Things are certainly not perfect. Otherwise we customers wouldn't grumble so much. But if someone could invent a process that, at very little cost, provided ways for companies to make more money, you'd want a part of it, wouldn't you?

So it follows that a readiness to elicit and pursue feedback would be a principal process in most businesses.

Let's move ourselves to WH Smith, in King's Cross station. To my untrained eye, there's a good team here, working well, particularly at very busy times. Many don't have English as a first language, but their politeness, courtesy and good humour would have already betrayed their foreign origins to most of us.

Now, like my colleague at Manchester United who has to coerce all those people into the stadium in less than 45 minutes, busy times do force focus on the 'basics'. You can't engage a football supporter in a ten-minute feedback exchange at the turnstile. Not without, at least, provoking a major disturbance and a barrage of sarcasm from further down the queue.

Equally, WH Smith experiences many busy periods so, to ensure the feedback is generated, it has installed a series of push buttons along the front of the counter, where customers may register a rating of service.

My travels show that this practice is proliferating, but does it work? Given my fascination with the subject I'm the first person to want to try this – I'll always give the time of day to a telephone researcher especially if it's a company after my feedback on their service – but I'm not sure I see many customers pushing the buttons. They're in too much of a hurry to catch their trains and cause a bottleneck in the buffet car with their ten-pound notes.

And yet, interesting news from South Africa reaches us. There, the practice of placing these automated feedback devices has been common for some time, particularly in banks and department stores.

While steps have been taken to prevent abuse by small children (and adults who think it's hilarious to press 'poor' repeatedly and run away), the experience has produced a surprising result. The presence of the devices keeps 'service' at the forefront of the employees' minds. So, whether or not the data being emptied from these machines is useful, their appearance has impacted positively on service regardless.

Perhaps this is the strategy in WH Smith. I applaud the fact that they appear to be focusing on service, and I'll even forgive them the bumpy ride.

It's one small step, as someone once famously said: a desperately necessary evolution from the inane grinning of employees who regard your attempts to help their business as a symptom of some kind of unsettling genetic disorder.

Elsewhere, we encounter the small feedback cards, the encouragement to provide us with ideas 'to improve our service to you' and even, as Moto Services has shown, additional little cards detailing exactly 'how we've responded to your feedback.'

This latter point is significant since we only know that

feedback is effective if the organisation receiving it does something differently as a result. Take for example the large UK retailer who regularly calls customers who have experienced their complaint handling process, to see what improvements the customer would suggest.

Originally, customers rated the complaint experience highly. However, in recent months, the scores have begun to fall, even though the investment in training and process improvement has increased. What has caused this?

Their belief is that customers are initially impressed with how seriously their concerns are greeted, but find that on subsequent visits to the organisation, the conditions that provoked the original complaint are still in evidence. For example, Betty still glowers at anyone raising the slightest polite concern and the response from staff to increasing queues at the till appears to be a mass exodus to the rest room.

I'm watching this organisation with interest, to see if these albeit blurred conclusions translate into tangible service improvements. I fear that most UK organisations who recognise the need for tangibility will focus on the 'look and feel', like the never-ending re-branding and re-styling of high street banks and building societies.

Some years ago, when I was working in the financial services industry, my employers carried out a survey to better understand what drove branch customers to rate the service. Given a list of several options the lowest element was reliability, not the 'look and feel'. And yet, by any measure, the lowest rated element was 'look and feel'. It's the least important factor. Which will explain the fact that so many millions of pounds are spent on the 'look and feel'. From coffee bars in the banking hall, to huge glass logos on Glasgow rooftops, it obviously matters to someone.

But not to me. I'm interested in the 'human' factors and I'm keen to give people feedback on this (in spite of my toy store experience).

So, at best, UK retail appears to be saying: feedback is welcome, but don't bet on many changes. At worst, it's crying out in some places, feedback isn't welcome at all.

So, as the snowdrops and crocuses peek from the ground and the cat rediscovers the art of spraying, springtime must surely bring some succour.

3

March

'Then give me the number of your Customer Services department so I can complain to them.'
'I can't. They don't take phone calls.'
Exchange overheard at department store cash desk in
Wolverhampton (March 2003).

The sucker, as it turns out, is me. Why? For actually believing the old chestnut that 'a complaint is a gift'. How many times have you heard that one trotted out by a desperate trainer on a customer service course at work?

Complaints, as we all know, are an occupational hazard sent by God to remind us of how pathetic a figure the hard-pressed employee cuts on this small windswept outpost. They are neither factored in to work time (as that would be an admission that mistakes are occasionally made) nor responded to positively (as that might suggest we're going to take you seriously and actually do something about the faulty blow torch that just turned your barbecue guests into a party pyre).

For the despondent employee facing a request to 'up the credit card leads' this week, the complicated root through last year's bank statements with Mr & Mrs Retired of Hastings is as welcome as a sharp kick in the Alberts.

For some, complaints are an opportunity to practise the opposite of ownership (tenancy, perhaps?) whereby the complaint is taken as a 'hot potato' and hurled across the room to the nearest, temporarily distracted employee or, worse still, used as an opportunity to blame someone else.

In some organisations, complaints are regarded as a personal snub. Getting those people to look at the comments objectively is impossible. It says I'm doing something wrong or that I'm not good at my job, when in fact it's the failure to record and take action that represents the dereliction of duty.

In some organisations, enthusiasm for dealing with complaints is illustrated perfectly by the way they organise 'complaint handling' as function. Check the names: 'Customer relations', 'Complaints' … not all inspiring. Most of us want someone who possesses a basic mastery of courtesy, feels a personal obligation to be honest and to take ownership of your problem and appears to have the power to put things right. Most of us encounter a harassed minion, two-thirds of the way from individual to clone, for whom you feel so much sympathy that the purpose of your call shifts from resolving your complaint to getting some counselling and support for the person with whom you are speaking.

And, on top of all of this, the diaspora of USA-originated customer service gems like 'it's a gift' and 'it's totally free service improvement feedback' begin to grate. Or do they?

But when you think about it, in these days of Internet shopping, mail order and telephone banking, personal contact has become more and more remote. Without the retail sector and its malls, department stores and out of town centres, there wouldn't be much human contact at all.

For organisations like **www.play.com** you only get to test how good their service is when something goes wrong. And in many ways this is a microcosm of the whole service issue. Getting the basics right – in effect, total mechanisation – requires no human interaction (apart from cursing the laptop or screaming 'I didn't want that' as your search for Bob Dylan's *Blonde on Blonde* throws up a particularly explicit interpretation of 'blonde on blonde'). The mechanisation plays to the need to remain remote: wanting to keep the purchase discreet, wanting to while away a few minutes at your desk reading reviews or wanting to price up a new washing machine.

But when things do go wrong (and surprisingly enough,

they do) it's the human interaction that, for me, determines just how successful these organisations are going to be. And that interaction only usually occurs when something goes wrong.

I use **www.play.com** to send a CD to my sister's boyfriend for his birthday. It hasn't arrived some two weeks later, despite the 'my account' page showing it left the day I ordered it. Helpfully the website explains that they do not normally pursue lost items until 14 days after the purchase.

Tentatively I call. Vicky, who answers, is politeness itself, warm and conversational. The bad news is that it's now out of stock, but we expect it in during the next 3-5 days and we'll send out the replacement immediately. I mention that it was for his birthday, to see if that generates a 'recorded delivery' and genuinely consider asking for my money back as he'll soon be a year older, but, all things considered, the query was welcome, I was treated well (though not exceptionally) and felt relatively obliged in spite of the lack of flexibility. **www.play.com** now has a human voice.

It was about another 10 days before the replacement arrived, which was the expectation set, so we're happy about that.

So, if my contention holds and human contact has become an endangered species, the complaint would naturally represent an excellent opportunity to demonstrate the value of continuing to do business with this organisation.

It's March 13 (my daughter's birthday) and we've booked well ahead on Virgin to travel by rail from Wakefield to Newcastle. Key to a successful trip is the need to have four seats together and, if a little too much to ask, that we be on the east side of the compartment when returning so my little lad can see the Tyne bridges and Durham Castle and Cathedral as we pass through God's own country. This, our operative had organised with grace and accuracy.

I like Virgin Trains. Not a common perception, I hear you shout from your abandoned siding in Coventry. But on the line from Bristol to Edinburgh all of the new Voyager trains are in service, you can plug your laptop in and the service is tangibly better than most other rail companies, at least in my recent memory.

The weekend passes off successfully and we begin our return journey. One of the four seats is occupied by a dour-looking woman, who at first looks away, when I politely ask her to move and then, as I insist, refuses point blank. Not used to such discourtesy, I continue to ask her to move. I have my wife and two children and we have booked ahead especially. 'Tough. I'm not moving. I've been here since Edinburgh,' she responds.

I make my under-the-breath comment as deliberately audible as possible: 'It's good to be reminded of the traditional warmth and generosity of the Scots again,' and march off to get assistance.

The assistant doesn't relish acting upon any of my suggestions but offers us accommodation in Club Class, should there be four seats together. There aren't, but we find a couple of spare pairs not too far from each other and sit stony-faced for the rest of the journey, punctuated by my childish and, I'm ashamed to say, audible prayers for her to suffer a painful demise.

When we get home and I have finally flicked a couple of despairing 'v's at her from the platform at Wakefield, I begin to feel disappointment at the way Virgin have handled the issue. However, putting myself in her shoes, I would have found it difficult to resort to physical coercion (as this appeared the only way the selfish passenger could be moved). But then again, the alternative offered wasn't suitable. I write to Virgin Trains.

After a week I receive an acknowledgement letter, stating that they are looking into my complaint. Several days after this I receive an apology, apparently, warm and understanding, with the hope that 'your little boy will enjoy the enclosed kid's pack and that it will make up for the inconvenience he suffered,' or words to that effect. Great, they see the point I was making: it was my little boy who missed out (and the entire family who has to put up with my pointless ranting thereafter) so they aim the compensatory gift at him. All very well, but someone has forgotten to enclose said kid's pack.

So another call and eventually, a couple of days later, a nice surprise for my little boy (who had by now forgotten the original issue) and some reassurance for Dad, who is currently working with a private detective agency in the hope of tracking down and 'taking out' our evil passenger. More on evil customers later – and their debilitating impact on levels of service in the UK.

I see this more enlightened approach in other travelling experiences with Virgin Trains, in spite of the problems our crumbling rail infrastructure hurls in their direction. On a trip to Edinburgh from Leeds we are sailing alongside the glorious ridge into Waverley Station ahead of time. The train manager, quick to see the opportunity, announces: 'With Michael Schumacher at the wheel, I'm pleased to say we are arriving into Edinburgh some 8 minutes early.' The conventional British steel breaks into a dozen smiles.

At this point the train shudders to a stop. There's a moment when we confidently expect it to resume its arrival.

The train manager again: 'Having arrived early, we have not yet been allocated a platform, so there may be a short wait before we complete our journey'. His tone betrays his despair at having risked a simple assumption when his destiny lay in the hands of the station management system.

Either way, it was almost reassuring. How many of his colleagues would have preferred to take a vow of respectful silence, rather than risking disappointment when all you were trying to do was to lighten hearts and show that you care?

Happily, this approach on Virgin Trains (at least on the east coast) appears to be by design, rather than by individual idiosyncrasy. On the way back we have a planned five-minute stop in Newcastle. The train manager, a delightfully cheerful lass called Karen, announces: 'for those of you who require an emergency nicotine break, you've just about enough time to leave the train for a couple of minutes, but please don't stray far.'

I'm encouraged by this general approach, especially as it tends not to reflect the experiences of my colleagues. Funnily enough, often involving the same organisation. When I meet with groups of employees and customers and ask them for their 'top ten' and 'bottom ten' UK organisations, Virgin Trains usually occupies the lower end of the scale. And yet this is largely provoked by the misery of regular travel on the west coast line, which, to my knowledge, is a combination of factors, many of which are beyond their influence or control.

Someone I recently met mentioned their Borough Council, who had clamped her car one morning because it was double-parked. This, in spite of her appealing (and not hearing back from the council) the original fine as all of the parking places had been taken by construction workers and residents had nowhere to park.

Oh yes, she'd been asked to pay by 9.00am on the morning the clamp was placed on the vehicle. She only saw the clamp as she left the house with her kids for the school journey.

One London Borough continues to fine a resident for crossing a bus lane. Fair enough, until you realise she has a bus lane between her drive and the main road. Each time she leaves the house, the camera whirrs into action, the ticket bounces on the doormat, she appeals and the labyrinthine process of trying to get blood out of a stone commences.

These straightforward cases do not require the wisdom of Solomon to resolve. Some, however, are much more testing. Take, for example, my mate, who lives in London and books an Apex fare to take in his favourite team's game. They play 'oop north' and, a few weeks before the game is due to take place, the match is re-arranged for the benefit of television. Realising that his Apex ticket is neither valid nor refundable for the new journey, he contacts the club for a refund of both ticket and travel costs. Your starter for ten: take a pencil and explain how the club should respond. The rulebook states that kickoff times can be altered up to and including kickoff time (crowd congestion, poor weather, security concerns, etc). So they're entitled to do it. But should they let the supporter lose out?

Organisations who acknowledge that their priorities often conflict with their customers' needs often fail to take into account that balancing interests is at the heart of a successful business. Successful businesses are built on an ability to make quick decisions. Empires are built in seconds, not over years. It takes seconds to deliver the promise but years to recover from a service disappointment.

We're back to ownership again and complaint management in the UK, while admittedly slowly getting its act together, fails to recognise one of the fundamental truths of good service: ownership results when the individual knows enough about what his or her organisation stands for (their values or strongly held traditions) and enough about the current local business context.

Question: how many businesses have designed the way they deal with complaints to reflect their values – however many bright posters around head office proclaim their importance?

Question: how many frontline staff get a chance to contribute to discussions about the company's performance, to offer opinions about what it could do to improve, develop and, heaven forbid, make life better for its employees? And where this does happen, is it more regular than once or twice a year?

I see a trend emerging when I discuss this with friends. One discovered his fresh chicken wasn't so fresh when he freed it from its wrapping. Upon taking it back to Tesco he was immediately given a replacement, without fuss or delay.

Another friend with an unhappy chicken returned his whence it came (on this occasion, from Asda) and, as previously mentioned, received a replacement chicken and a full refund of the original price.

In each of these organisations, a conscious process is

being played out. You sense that the arrival of a complaint or a customer concern generates a process that is as part of 'business as usual' as checking in deliveries or picking up a wage cheque. Elsewhere, complaint management (and in most places, customer service in its entirety) comes across as something people do when they have time or when other work is finished.

I'm reminded of an attempt to have a family Christmas meal at a family-dining pub in South Yorkshire. Having booked ahead, we arrive to be told that the place is so busy, there may be a wait of up to half an hour between courses. This, as it turns out, was akin to telling the residents of east London during the blitz that they might hear a small bang.

Now in the circumstances, we might decide to abandon a course, or go elsewhere to eat, if we are given an honest appraisal of just how long we are going to have to wait. Several items of my sister's wardrobe go out of fashion during the period between starters and main course.

At a couple of points during the meal, I venture a question about when the main courses were going to arrive. Eventually I raise the possibility that the establishment might wish to take something off the cost of the meal for our discomfort and inconvenience (we have four children with us who have finished their starters some 90 minutes before the mains arrive). The refusal from the lady at the till was as flat as her Yorkshire burr.

We leave extremely disappointed with the service and determined to put our complaint in writing since no one at the establishment seems to care. Some 14 days later I receive a personal apology from the office of the chief executive, with the total value of the meal refunded in vouchers. But why does it take so long and so much hassle to extract the apology? The woman who served us clearly appeared keener to slide her finger down the cheese slicer than to release the phrase 'We're sorry'.

I calculate the cost of this process from the impact on the likelihood of customers revisiting the establishment to the management time in resolving the problem. I believe the organisation has the customer's best interests at heart, but perhaps they could learn from the Asian hotel group whose management team attribute their success to the fact that 'our people have to ask their manager's permission to say NO to a customer.'

You know, I once queued in a Prêt branch in Oxford Street, picked up a sandwich and ordered a latte. 'The latte's on us' said the boy at the till. 'I saw how long you had to queue.'

The 'Real Madrid' of the service world could teach much to the family diner – where at least its senior people recognise the value of dealing with complaints effectively (but don't have the courage to devolve this authority and, more importantly, attitude, to the front line).

I think I've made the case that some complaints are testing. Some gnaw away at that frayed piece of rope at the centre of the tug-o-war between the organisation's interests and those of its customers. Some are successful: they chew through, snap the rope and send the organisation spinning away from its bemused and bewildered customers.

Another problem with complaints is their occasional ferocity. Most retailers will be faced with animated customers on a fairly regular basis, but sometimes, the intimidation and aggression from the customer is unwarranted. While conflict training is a recommended and, in some industries, a necessary investment, employees shouldn't be abandoned by organisations.

And yet, I see comparatively few organisations following GNER's lead with prominent posters explaining that they will not tolerate aggressive and/or abusive behaviour from passengers. I support this because it works at two levels: first, it defends the staff by addressing the problem before it arises ('if you were thinking of taking it out on our people, think again') but secondly, and more importantly in my view, it shows 'your people' that you care about them. It's a symbol of the value the organisation places in its own people.

Ditto the 'look and feel' of a retail outlet. Not important to customers, perhaps, but very important for the comfort and motivation of its employees.

Sadly, however, frontline employees appear to be left to fend for themselves when problems arise and, for every inspired moment of ownership, there's a basketful of broken promises and futile correspondence.

I go surfing to check out the price of a particular printer I need. It's an Epson (not the racecourse, stupid) and once I happen upon a price tidy enough for my tight pockets, I commit and await its arrival. It arrives, is plugged in and stubbornly refuses to burst into frenzied printing action. At which point I raise my concerns with the manufacturers, who immediately (well, the next day) dispatch an engineer to come out and help me.

He quickly diagnoses the problem ('It doesn't work') and nips out to the van to find a replacement machine for me. Once he's sure I'm happy that the replacement machine works, he takes his leave while I pop back into my home office to engage in some serious printing. At which point my eyes are drawn to the package on the table. It's an Epson 'sorry pack'. It contains some 'freebie' printing material and resources and software and materials for printing kids' tee shirts. I like it. How did he know I have kids? (The lack of hair and the haggard look, perhaps).

It's a nice touch with an apologetic letter explaining their pride in their product and their understanding of our disappointment when it doesn't work.

I'm now a fully subscribed Epson fan (although I'm still looking for a way to express my love for them, short of energetically deflowering my printer). But let's analyse what they've done. It's cost comparatively little to provide this pack as it all comes from stock they maintain in large quantities. It doubles as a neat piece of promotion for some of the other products they sell. It's easy and relatively cheap for them to give and it means a lot to the complaining customer.

Anyone else got this approach? I ask myself as I caress my feeder. Some months later, it happened again. On this occasion we had been wondering what to do with our wheelie bin. You push it out onto the main road and it's collected each Thursday. That would be the normal protocol, but we're about to go away for a fortnight in Spain. If we leave it out for week one, it'll be there until week two. Without wishing to cast nasturtiums on other residents, this does signal our absence and may lead to some rogue deducing that we might represent an ideal burgling opportunity.

So, having weighed up the pros and cons we decided to leave the wheelie bin just inside our drive, so that the bin men wouldn't see it from the end of the street, but would notice its presence as they passed by and process it.

Perhaps the seafood barbecue we had the night before we left for Spain was not the best idea. Inevitably, the steaming bin was still there to greet us when we returned a fortnight later, surrounded by several engorged cats, looking like extras from Babette's feast.

Having concluded that the three inches separating the bin from the road would somehow excuse the bin men from taking it, we contacted the council by email to vent our frustration (having apologised to the neighbours for the distressing smell of fish emanating from our drive).

What was to follow restored my faith. Having had an emailed acknowledgement to the complaint and, frankly, having forgotten about it a couple of days later, there was a knock at the door. Imagining a visit from the friends of Mr Jehovah, I marched towards the door, rehearsing my excuses ('my spirituality is a private thing. Now bugger off').

I was greeted by a manager from the local Refuse Collection Department, who introduced himself and explained that he and the junior colleague alongside him were carrying out a regular visit to discuss service with the residents in this part of West Yorkshire. 'My Customer Relations people tell me you have an outstanding complaint, so I wondered if I could help.'

Outstanding? My complaint probably wasn't, but this response was. Again, it all made perfect sense. On the one hand, keep talking to your residents, keep the lines of communication open and issues like mine would be picked up as concerns before they become complaints, and then, through dialogue and discussion, faith is sustained, instead of needing to be restored.

Not only that, but having such well-oiled internal communication channels (as they obviously have) meant that they could give the impression of a joined-up organisation – not something for which councils are generally renowned.

People tell me there's a huge gap between the leadership of large businesses and frontline staff – and therein lies the entire issue. There shouldn't be. In physical terms, the leaders should be on the front line regularly enough to understand the environment in which customers are being served. They should make 'back to the floor' exercises a requirement before bonuses can be paid. In many cases a knife between the ribs would be more deserving than a golden handshake for some departing executives.

Secondly, why should leadership only occupy the realm of the farts in suits at the top? I'm not about to embark on the old management vs. leadership debate which you've all heard before, but why is the customer's experience more often than not a result of too much emphasis on management and not enough on leadership? Staff behave the way they behave because of what they've been told to do. Frontline employees are not encouraged to discuss solutions openly – the leaders impose solutions upon them in the business.

One great Chinese philosopher said that 'a great leader walks behind his people'. In some UK organisations, they'll be about 20 miles behind their people. Like Field Marshal Haig and the Tommy on the front line – only linked by distant hierarchy – not by belief.

Where the organisation's employees appear to share beliefs and are actively encouraged to bring them into play when difficult situations occur, I expect we customers would see a lot more balanced decision-making, more acceptance of 'grey areas', more flexibility and less indifference.

There are some employees who deserve to be moved on because of their appalling attitudes, but we mustn't rush to condemn the individual out of hand, when the majority of experiences I suffer simply reflect an organisation that doesn't create clarity of purpose for its frontline people.

This morning I pay a cheque into the local agency of my bank. I count seven different posters and leaflets effectively summarising the 'rules'. We can't draw cash from the till with such and such an account; we can only use the ATM outside. We have to do this, we must do that, they won't do this, they can't do that. There's even a complaints leaflet telling us what we 'must' do if we wish to raise a complaint with them. I receive neither a smile nor a welcome when I enter the agency.

I was aching for acknowledgement – a smile or a line about the weather. You could have laughed at my lack of hair or told me what you had for breakfast. Sometimes I mouth 'I love you' while staring them in the eyes. Watch the reaction you get. It keeps you sane.

What would have been nice would have been to see a poster telling us 'what we CAN do', 'what we WILL do when you have a problem', 'why you are important to us' etc. Nothing of the sort. And banks wonder why customers don't like them.

There's a bank in the USA that tells its customers it is a 'retailer'. Simple enough, but it makes their people think like retailers and, funnily enough, recognise that success is built upon customer service. Commerce Bank, for that is its name, has rules so tight that they squeak. 'How may I help you?' is encouraged and is fine, but 'How CAN I help you?' gets the individual a little constructive feedback, if you know what I mean.

One major UK building society knows that its customers' commitment to stay loyal and invest more with them is more likely to be driven by its employees' attitudes than its relative convenience, accessibility and range of products.

So where else have I complained, you're asking. Strangely enough, in few places. Not because the service has been good everywhere, but because complaining appears to be pointless.

Wouldn't it be nice, once in a while, to be asked by the cashier, 'As we're quiet, do you have five minutes to tell me about the service you receive from us?'?

The skies are darkened by a formation of pigs.

4

April

'I'm afraid it fell off the order shelf'
Explanation given for late arrival of coffee at hotel in
Leicestershire (April 2003).

For the continental reader, April welcomes in spring and the Sunday morning aperitif moves outdoors, as the orange blossom perfumes the renewed garden, finches descend for seeds and the children frolic on the lawn.

Unfortunately, for the UK reader, the only movement detectable in the garden at this time of year is the furtive rustling of next door's cat, looking for somewhere to poo amidst the jagged shards of frosted soil.

Having recently given a talk on the subject of defining service, I seek examples to prove my contention as I go about my day. It's not an earth-shattering revelation, this contention. I simply go along with the majority of the evidence, which shows that service can be split, by and large, into two elements. On the one hand you have the basics: those elements relating to opening hours, access, quality of product, price, functionality and reliability. A good example would be 'queuing' in shops and banks. Where the queues are managed well, no problem. When they aren't, it begins to suggest that the basics are a bit weak.

On the other hand you have all of the often intangible human factors, from a feeling that this person genuinely has your best interests at heart to displays of ownership, humour, courtesy and respect, irrespective of the organisation you are dealing with.

•

I have just come off the phone from a chat with an assistant at the One Account. It's been a pleasure. I got the information I wanted (the website was down) and the person I spoke to had the time to share a joke, a couple of observations and wish me well. When I analyse it, the experience was all the better for the website being down. The 'basics' were lacking, just this once, but the human factor more than made up for this. Service was 0-3 down at half time and reduced to ten men, but recovered to win 4-3 with a goal in the last minute.

It strikes me that we rarely see the human factor at work when we 'shop' in the UK, or at least, at those national chains and larger stores. Processes have been sharpened and streamlined, costs have been squeezed out and technology has made every interaction just as easy over the web as it would be face to face.

The cumulative impact of all of this modernisation has been to reduce our exposure to human contact. And yet, as all the evidence shows, the human contact is the hidden weapon of mass arousal that we all want to believe in, even if this obliges the appearance of yet another dangling preposition.

But I'm out on the street intent on human contact. Let me clarify (as I had to do for the policeman's benefit when he overheard me state this in Briggate in Leeds) that I'm referring to an intended bout of shopping in central Leeds (rather than paying for female companionship). And if you're expecting me to produce a diatribe on service levels in the massage parlour industry, think again (it's in hand).

The food and drink retail industry does bear scrutiny. Leisure is rapidly becoming central to most lives. However, leisure, a word that conjures up images of relaxing and refreshment, apparently relates to extreme tobogganing, ice mountain climbing and generally moving around far quicker than is good for my delicate little body.

Leisure is therefore a growth industry. The more I relax the larger I become, incidentally. You would imagine that it would have built service into its offerings. After all, service is part of the mix required to gain a Michelin star.

And yet, as someone not generally afforded the luxury of eating in such an environment, I'm going to focus on the places I'm likely to visit.

Perhaps the hotel subscribes to a pamphlet I received unsolicited in the post the other day. It purported to show employees how to deal with employee law and, among other things, 'find out if your people are pregnant' as, they reliably inform me, 'you've found your ideal recruit, who has the necessary skills and attitude to fulfil the position you desperately need to fill. But if you're going to spend lots of money on training and induction, how do you find out if the recruit is pregnant?'

Amazing. My advice would be that male recruits are not generally going to cause difficulties. But read on: 'ask if she is currently dealing with a doctor or any other medical profession. In this way, she will be obliged to concede that she is in the care of a midwife and you can review your decision.'

I paraphrase, but it's easy to see why employees in the UK provide underwhelming levels of service if this approach to employee relations were to prevail.

Our odyssey takes us to Sheffield: the Division Street quarter, hugely transformed from my student days there in the early 80s into a vibrant centre of activity, combining the mysterious delights of the 'Rare and Racy' second-hand bookstore and the Forum: a brilliant collection of clothes shops.

My beloved and I had brought our kids along and, given our penchant for relaxing, decided to take a reviving drink in the nearest pub. It had an outside, first floor patio area, that you access from the back and which, incidentally, was completely void of customers, apart from us. We settled down and I went in to get the drinks. My daughter followed me in excitedly, anticipating a bag of crisps (we know how to live).

'Am I OK with the kids outside?' I asked, at the risk of inviting problems. 'We're just here for a drink.'

'Sorry, but kids can't come in unless you're having a full meal and they're eating too.'

'But it's 4 o'clock. We don't want to eat yet.'

'Then I can't serve you. Kids can only come in if they're having a substantial meal.'

Thus began my boycott of this establishment: an organisation on the point of tapping into the continental approach of welcoming families and benefiting from both their cash and their future patronage. We have never been back since, in spite of children's meals being effectively given away there.

I've since had a chat with someone who knows the organisation well. They were able to set out the quandary very clearly, explaining that the move to allow children had upset a fair few customers; hence (and probably not the only reason) their appearances would be restricted to lunchtime eating. There are also archaic licensing laws in this country that apparently allow three-year-old to toss back gin and tonic, as long as someone else orders it.

But the company behind the pub is built soundly on delighting the customer, so maybe our experience was a function of the organisation experimenting, finding that things haven't worked out and needing to maybe step back on that 'children only at lunchtime' thing and abandoning the concept altogether. A year later the 'substantial meal' sign still hangs outside that establishment. Do you know anyone who can get their kids to eat a substantial meal? Especially one containing vegetables?

I hope they abandon the concept and go either way: no kids or all kids, because you can never overestimate the impact on a family of being told to finish your drink and move on.

But, whether it's an antiquated rule or a lack of business nous or even, perhaps, the assorted detritus of society strewn about the place objecting to kids in adjacent patios, I don't really understand the UK's problem with children.

But my kids are hardy souls. Many's the time they have to put up with Dad grumbling about some aspect of service, but it's obviously been effective as they are beginning to see what all the fuss is about.

Compare this experience with an event in Durham the following weekend. April is a cold month and the northeast can be unforgiving for the promenading family group.

My son, who was 7 at the time, was complaining that once the coffee shops start to close from around 5pm onwards, there's nowhere for a family to go for a drink 'just like they do in Spain'. Quite rightly, the family ethos of Mediterranean countries is generally manifested as mid-evening strolls, pre-lunch family gatherings and a general love of kids.

Just as we had decided to call it a day, we noticed a new place had opened just down from the University: Brown Sugar. From the outside it was an intriguing sight. At the extreme left it had sofas, satellite TV with sports and a general 'bar' atmosphere. In the centre it appeared to be a restaurant and to the right, a coffee bar, with a range of pastries, yer pot of olives and warmed pitta bread, etc.

It even had a small patio to the extreme left and, although temperatures were plummeting, our low level of expectation led me to enter and enquire as to whether the family (grandparents, parents and a 7- and 4-year-old) could sit outside and have a drink.

'Don't sit out there,' came the reply, 'bring them in. You'll freeze.'

'You sure?' I retorted, waiting for the oasis to evaporate.

'Of course.'

It all became clear with the appearance of an Italian man, who emerged with a couple of lollypops for my kids. His assistant, the very same girl who had greeted us, asked me if the kids wanted to see their aquarium.

We ordered olives, pitta bread, crisps, one extra dry martini, two tiger beers (to remind my Dad of his military service in Malaya), a cappuccino, some orange juice and a cinnamon steamer.

Part of the time was spent describing our delight at coming across a place that was so obviously clear about the opportunity presented by the general derision aimed at kids in this country. If they're not interested in mutant chicken shapes and tasteless processed ice cream, you've had it.

Our bill was about £15 and I recall we left the change from a twenty, as a tip. Now, being a naturalised Yorkshireman, that says something.

When we've gone north to visit my parents, we've been back. And before putting this experience in writing, I've told lots of people.

I don't pretend that the Sheffield pub and Brown Sugar operate in the same market. I accept that. I would just like pub and restaurant owners to give some thought to the financial possibilities of focusing on the family. I am not advocating a wholesale welcoming of kids into every drinking establishment, but pointing out that there is money to be made by addressing the lack of provision.

There's room for everyone. No kids to kids welcome. But what we're finding on our trip is a number of places who want to have their cake and eat it. Or who literally want our kids to have very nasty cake, eat it, pay well over the odds for it and clear off immediately afterwards. Brown Sugar does more than the minimum and appears to appeal to everyone. I hope it prospers and I hope the competition learns from it.

Brown Sugar offers an environment in which, over time, kids can come to appreciate socialising. It's a promising antidote to the society which keeps wine and beer, even in tiny diluted amounts, away from kids until their teens, at which point (or, indeed, pint) the sudden windfall of booze leads to the vomiting hordes in our city centres. It brings a touch of Mediterranean warmth to our cold streets, to replace the liquid laughs lining the sick-gilded doorways of the British city centre pub.

The experience confirms the existence of two main service precepts: the basics and the human factor. By 'basics' I'm referring to what the experts call 'hygiene factors': those fundamental promises of the service proposition. For a pub or restaurant, it relates to access, opening times, prices, food and drink quality, interior design and washroom quality, etc.

The companies I know have found that you can't ignore these basics. They represent minimum expectations and their presence or absence is likely to have a huge bearing on how successful your business is.

However, UK companies who are interested in service have discovered, by and large, that their impact on customers' perceptions is not as strong as the 'human' factor: that elusive spark of humanity that shows that the person you are dealing with has your best interests at heart. My experience is that UK companies focus on the former to the detriment of the latter. They also manage to translate this lack of awareness to the employer/employee relationship as the following example attests.

Investment in bank branch interiors in the mid-90s, I once discovered, hugely outweighed investment in service. One bank admitted to me that it was investing a quarter of a million pounds in upgrading one of its flagship branches; while staff at the same locale pointed out that their toilets had been the only area unaffected by these improvements. The same bank discovered that of all the subsets of the service definition, 'the look and feel' (i.e. that area they spent the most on) was the aspect rated least important by its customers (with 'reliability' conversely, emerging as the most important).

Among the other establishments we visit during April is Café Rouge. Here (in the Ecclesall Road restaurant in Sheffield) we are greeted by attentive staff. Bit by bit their strategy emerges. Initially smiling, being incredibly flexible, offering alternatives, smiling again, greeting requests as if it's a pleasure and positively purring at the slightest issue, as if problem resolution were the point of differentiation.

If I had to guess, I'd say the team there were trying to increase footfall. I'd guess the manager briefs the team regularly on what they need to do to make the restaurant a success. Much of the effort is clearly on the 'basics', as the complexities of the restaurant business demand, but equal emphasis is placed on putting the customer at ease, removing any potential seeds of discomfort and creating an atmosphere conducive to relaxation and enjoyment.

The day my son makes his First Confession, we decide to introduce an appropriate celebration: a seafood lunch. While the Catholics among you try to recall where lobster fits into the sacrament of reconciliation, let me describe the experience at Livebait in Leeds. Livebait resides in the Calls quarter of Leeds, where, in the recent past, people used to watch the progress of shopping trolleys floating down the Aire. How things have changed. There are new developments, trendy bars and the first million-pound flat was recently sold there, for people who are now able to lean against their stainless steel balcony railings and watch the shopping trolleys float by.

Having made the short trip to Leeds, dressed to the tens and eager to eat fish, we had arrived a little early. However, the warmth of the welcome when the door was opened was infectious. The seafood wasn't, thankfully, and we enjoyed a wonderful lunch, characterised particularly by the attention paid to my kids.

Other parents will appreciate that the pens given to the kids actually worked; the 'how to eat a lobster' sheet of paper was truly engaging and the invite to my five-year-old daughter to accompany the waitress to the bar for a look at the fresh seafood was as delightful as it was unexpected.

My kids tucked into cod and chips and, when we finally left, I was genuinely surprised to learn that we had spent more than two hours in the restaurant (I had been hoping for the waitress to invite me back for a look around too).

Livebait is part of a larger restaurant group – and clearly an organisation with its eye on the ball. Unsurprisingly, there were feedback cards presented with the bill. Thoughtfully designed and easy to complete. My email address for some fair feedback? A fair exchange. I scribbled down my positive impressions. We made a pact to return. More expensive than Café Rouge, but another class altogether. Food and service combined. Flexibility and focus. Family values and, I pray, an improving bottom line.

My improving waistline is also testament to our patronage of Pizza Hut. A different market from Café Rouge and Livebait – where a family emerge some £70-80 lighter – Pizza Hut scores points for consistency. Wherever you visit a Pizza Hut, the experience is broadly similar. 'Basics', such as the choice and taste of food, the layout and the price, represent an invisible consistency: one that, from the customer's perspective, drives neither increased visits nor increased expenditure. Where Pizza Hut appears to have the edge[2], however, is on the consistency of delivery of a good customer experience.

Where the activities at McDonalds are measured by the second, Pizza Hut pay equal attention to speed of service. No sooner had our starters disappeared, the pizza arrived. Actually, on this occasion, the pizza arrived sooner than our starters had disappeared. At one point I settled back into my seat and began to imagine myself in a Keystone Cops movie, everyone waddling around at double speed, poised to make sure there's no 'empty table time'.

'Is everything all right?' piped the young waitress to a quartet of chewing customers.

I begin to suspect that Pizza Hut have got this down to a fine art. Speed, food and price constitute a combination – an overall experience – for which people drop by. I understand that the company assiduously records performance against this experience – through mystery shopping and customer research maybe – and finds that the branches delivering the experience most consistently, experience the greater increase in traffic.

Which brings me to Prêt à Manger. An organisation initially lauded for its commitment to the freshest products, made daily on the premises. As a native of the northeast, my sub-

---

[2] Forgive the pun, but I'm expecting a van-load of cheesy bread in return

conscious mind presents a number of traditional offerings at times of extreme hunger. It amuses me to list those that would have pride of place twenty years ago: a Gregg's cheese and onion stottie, a ham and pease pudding sandwich, a huge lump of Cheddar with sixty-eight cream crackers. These days, probably only the stottie remains, trying to stop the crayfish and rocket sandwich from barging its way to the front.

I visit Prêt à Manger on my way to clients in Kensington. I've arrived an hour early for my meeting, so I plan a houmous wrap and a bag of those syrup-coated almonds. I consider the calorie level to be insufficiently 'girlie' so opt for a latte too – an extra strong one.

The young, Mediterranean, tanned server pours a sparkling smile in my direction and trots off my order over his shoulder to the expresso machine man, setting off an amusing exchange of light-hearted comments. I smile back. I'm happy. I settle back in the corner and recall previous visits to Prêt.

The first visit, in London's Oxford Street, I've already mentioned in an earlier chapter. 'The latte's on us, sir,' came the reply. 'I saw how long you had to queue.'

Did I actually experience that or is it apocryphal? Apocryphal? I can hear my Mum telling me, 'If it's apocryphal, I would put some calamine lotion on it.'

On another occasion the family made its first visit to the Prêt in Leeds. Cool, eh? We call it Prêt. We shorten it to welcome it into our world. Maybe that's why Dixons doesn't fare so well.

It was late afternoon – a Saturday, I guess – and there were few people left in the shop. My children were perched on those stools that are so high, Vodafone could have negotiated the installation of a mobile phone mast in one of the legs. A polite young Frenchman served us.

'Excuse me. We have a new range of muffins today and still have plenty left. Would your children like to take some home with them?'

Is the Pope Catholic? Do bears, (etc.)? Now we can't walk past Prêt without my kids suggesting we pop in.

The well briefed will be aware that Prêt regularly donate their remaining stock to local shelters and homelessness organisations, neatly clearing their shelves with a note of generosity. How nice to see a nice family-focused twist on this.

Accustomed as I am to wandering the streets of London before the shops open, I have often noticed staff meetings in Prêt branches. So it's all planned!

'Lads!' the barman shouts. 'We're launching a new beer here today and haven't sold it all. Would you like to take some home with you – for free?'

I wake up.

I end my foodie April on a cold morning on the M62. Birchwood services – and in need of some breakfast. Pity the souls who have to work at Birchwood, as, especially on the westbound side, the facilities haven't changed much since the sixties. When compared with some of the newer facilities, such as Tibshelf, on the M1 (J28), it falls way behind. But I know the 'look and feel' doesn't matter and anyway, I'm not here to marvel at the architecture, I'm here for fried egg on toast.

What a friendly team. Plenty of banter – food made to order – and a tasty breakfast. The 'basics' might be lacking, in terms of the aforementioned 'look and feel', but the working atmosphere the team has created more than compensates. Elsewhere on Britain's motorways, stopping by for a snack can be a dark affair at best. Birchwood may be crumbling, but it's the apple of my eye this April.

All in all, there's evidence that many UK eating and drinking establishments have begin to consider the 'human' factor and have started to design their organisations to deliver it.

And it has a monetary value. The more relaxed and at ease the diner is, the more likely a dessert will be purchased. Maybe not the most scientific theory I have ever produced, but I think it holds water.

As well as water, the waiters at Da Sandro in Huddersfield carry in sparklers for kids celebrating birthdays. Nothing special in that respect, but it's the other, almost incidental factors that create the stress-free environment.

We enter the restaurant to celebrate my son's First Holy Communion: my wife and I, our two kids, both of my sisters and their three kids, one of whom, Jack, uses a wheelchair to get around and another, Dylan, who has reached the ripe old age of 15 months and has seen the entertainment value of throwing pasta at people. Ruby, aged 2 months at the time, quietly observes the chaos around her, making a mental note of the arm trajectory required to spray bolognese sauce at the earliest opportunity.

Two highchairs are immediately produced. Again, what you'd expect. But then two other waiters approach the table to speak to my sisters and 'coo' their youngest. The stress melts away from them, eyes light up and the scene is prepared for a successful celebration.

It's 'pudding power', you know. This happens and you buy a pudding. We didn't, as it happens, favouring several strong expressos to carry us through the afternoon, but the bill equalled the national debt of Argentina, so we believe that Da Sandro shall remain prosperous still.

Da Sandro is clearly not alone in understanding how to create conditions for a relaxed meal, especially for a family with young kids. And virtually every other Italian restaurant stands apart from its competition through 'pudding power'.

5

May

'I can personally guarantee that the only reason I need your telephone number is to be able to let you know if you have won our raffle.

We won't be trying to sell you anything.'

Door-to-door salesman at my house (Day 1)

'This service will only cost you a few pence a day.'

Telephone salesperson (Day 2)

This security company is not alone in discovering the delights of telephone selling. If this market hasn't reached saturation point, I don't know what has. On average I receive several calls a week, mostly to sell me critical illness packages. In fact, there have been so many that I look over my shoulder when I leave the house, in case something nasty happens and they ring back to say, 'We told you so.'

I'm not against outbound selling. There's a time and a place ('never' and 'somewhere else' please). But it's slowly producing a tide of resentment amongst UK residents, especially when the caller won't get off the phone.

Added to that is the frustrating experience of hearing the distant 'beep' of the computer when you pick up – and no voice. We all know the technology scans the directories and rings your number. Unfortunately, the same zeal that drives investors to engage in this pointless marketing is also reflected in the failure to provide sufficient numbers of people to make the calls.

Today's breakfast TV reports that some individuals get up to 200 calls a day in that fashion. Call me extreme, but they should be able to return the favour and call the company 200 times a day and then hang up (deleted curse).

Jerry Seinfeld has the best solution. When you receive an unwelcome sales call, invoke the following emergency procedure:

'Thanks, but it's not convenient now. Could you give me your home number so I can ring you back and talk to you about it later?'

'I'm afraid we don't give out home numbers.'

'Why? Is that because you don't want a complete stranger ringing you at home and selling you something you don't want?'

'Er … yes.'

But when they ask you to provide feedback – please give them your time.

One of the most frustrating aspects is the fact that they won't tell my wife why they want to speak to me, only that it has to be me to whom they speak. Why go to all the trouble when my wife is perfectly able to tell them to piss off too (and that I'm sorry I've missed the payment, the cheque's in the post).

Recent experiences paint a wide and wonderful landscape of the rich pasture that is outbound calling. Monday afternoon, 1pm, and I'm hunched over my laptop deep in concentration. What was that website that lets you design and send your own cards again?

The phone rings. It's Volkswagen. That's where I got my car – and to whom most of my income is regularly handed. The call opens positively with a few questions to identify me as one of their customers and to explain that they are simply calling to ask me for feedback on the recent service my car had received. It would take about ten minutes.

Impressed by the chance to explain how one of the staff keeps interrupting the others when they're with customers (i.e. me), I gave of my time, supplied my opinions and ratings, indicated the likelihood of re-purchasing another Volkswagen (that Euro Lottery has got to pay off sometime) and we sailed sweetly to a conclusion: Volkswagen apparently content with some descriptive (and, I have to say, generally very positive) feedback, and me feeling that, for once, the company was interested in the process of driving sales – my experience as a customer – rather than simply ringing me up and selling things to me.

Not two minutes later the phone rang again and this time it was a national car repair chain. Now I like them. The team at my local branch are excellent. Not only do they provide quick and reliable service but they're nice to you. I used to think it was because of the picture of their founder and MD placed strategically behind every reception desk. Not necessarily that he was making strong customer commitments on the poster, but maybe because of the implied beating the team would get if they failed in their endeavours. Only joking, but it works at my local store (and the poster's gone).

The caller wanted to check that I had had a tyre repaired on the previous Saturday. I settled back intent on providing the same detailed feedback on what had been an excellent service, quick, reliable and very inexpensive. I wanted to tell them that they are the Shangri La of the motoring world. Men like me (i.e. girly men) want our cars to run smoothly without servicing or the need ever to open the bonnet. That Saturday I had punctured my tyre in my own drive and the traditional sequence of events played out.

First, fighting back the tears, I explain that we have a puncture and our family's entire weekend, if not month, will be ruined. With an understanding and patient smile, my wife guides the kids into the living room ('Daddy will be OK soon'). I then return to the car to weep inconsolably for 40 minutes, after which I take out the manual.

Several minutes later my wife reappears, takes the manual and starts the process of changing the wheel. Guiltily, I join in. It starts to rain. I start to cry again. My wife provides an anorak for me. After several minutes only, we remove the bolts. At this point we discover that the wheel has corroded and can't easily be removed from the axle (I had to look up the terminology here).

My wife suggests a friend who knows about these things (i.e. any other member of the public). I protest. 'It's the weekend. How can we do this to him?' He turns out to be at home, looking for excuses not to tidy up the house while his wife is at the hairdressers. Steve is happy to come around. He whacks off the wheel with a plank of wood, supported by a central jack and in no time we're on our way for the repair.

But on the phone, now, I don't get the chance to explain how happy I was that the garage told me I didn't need a new tyre. The puncture was at the bottom, in the tread, and could be repaired. They simply asked me if I was happy with the service; what else they could do to improve and then … if I would give them the renewal date of my car insurance so they could send me a quote. 'You just haven't earned it yet, Baby,' as Morrissey once sang.

Funny how these calls always come in at 1.00 in the afternoon. It's become a curiously reassuring heartbeat in this household.

Based on the anecdotes of people I come across, there are two noticeable trends in this form of perceptions collection. First, and thankfully, is an increase in the ratio between service calls and sales calls. A year ago, every unwanted call was trying to sell me something. Now, a growing percentage of calls are aimed at collecting my feedback in what appears to be a genuine attempt to improve their service and get more of us to spend more – or at least stay loyal to the brand.

That many of these calls are thinly disguised sales calls is worrying. Worrying, because the behaviour of the naughty few taints perceptions of the genuine ones. Worrying, because it demonstrates the extent to which UK organisations misunderstand service. It's not service and sales – two different outputs. It's sales through service: sales as an output of customer-focused service delivery.

So what are these organisations doing with the information they receive from these surveys? Well … not as much as you would hope.

The first category of organisations covers those who don't even ask their own customers what they think of their service. There are far more of these companies than you would imagine. Some companies at the other end of the spectrum ask their competitors' customers for opinions – so some know what everyone thinks and some, like Manuel in *Fawlty Towers*, know naaatheeng.

The second category telephone or write to customers to ask for ratings and commitment intention. This can be extremely useful, but for most organisations engaged at this level, appears to be a process whereby:

- Senior managers and market researchers develop a questionnaire (with or without customer input)
- Questionnaires are sent out or phone calls made to customers (usually by a third party who does this for a bunch of other organisations too)
- Feedback is collated; presented to wide group of senior managers at Head Office
- Er … that's it
- Oh, well possibly there'll be a change in products some years down the line
- And, most definitely, any changes will be imposed on frontline employees

How, precisely, does this drive improvement for customers? Very imprecisely, I would venture.

The third category of organisations are interested in improvement, because, apparently, they believe that continuous interaction with customers is fundamental to keeping the money coming in.

Their part of the rainbow is characterised by a greater degree of practicality and common sense – and unencumbered by conventional research protocols. It goes something like this:

- The surveying approach features input from managers, researchers, customers and, heaven forbid, frontline colleagues
- The calls are made by people responsible for (or having great influence over) customer service or, if it's a paper survey, the survey asks customers to provide verbatim comments, preferably on something that has recently happened
- It happens often enough to enable the organisation to act quickly if something appears to be going wrong
- Customers are not constrained by ridiculous average handling times but encouraged to provide stories, narrative, little gems, etc., that the caller can use as a springboard for further discussion
- Top-level suggestions, ratings and ideas can still be generated for senior management – and for some of the valid exercises that it will generate
- However, improvement ideas are passed to the front line so that they can be discussed and actioned
- There is even one UK organisation that I know of that passes the survey forms back to its frontline colleagues so they can contact customers who may have made specific comments about the service those very people provide

I'm not debunking conventional approaches here, but speaking as a UK customer and questioning their relevance as a sole intervention. If you're really interested in customer service, and if you really believe what you tell your institutional investors, then show me how the conventional approach impacts on frontline service improvements.

Now it comes to pass, that as I become distracted by the news from Sunderland AFC's website that a little egret has been spotted at their training academy (and, as I write, that our star player has been stung by a jellyfish during a training session), I receive a home visit. Here's a topic not many customer service gurus ever attempt to handle. Why? Mostly because the successful ones have escaped into the seclusion of the wealthier belts, where their guard dog (Zoltan, hound of Dracula) keeps the Jehovahs at bay. Me? I'm here south of Bradford, not a hundred yards from a busy junction and well in the sights of 'home visitor'.

I've learned to categorise visitors to the house, but found technique sadly lacking. Even I would be prepared to buy an alarm system if I thought the guy was genuinely trying to establish if I needed one, but finding someone prepared at least to answer your questions is as likely as a programme on television or radio that doesn't feature a contribution from Stuart Maconie.

An alarm system capable of pre-warning you of an impending sales visit might actually be a popular seller, come to think of it.

First up, the Jehovah's Witnesses. A smart suit in my street immediately raises suspicion. Either I'm in court (up for shop assistant abuse again) or God's emissaries are abroad. In earlier times I'd be engaged in discussion for a little while before taking a magazine and wishing them well. More recently, however, I've countered their rising fundamentalism with a sharp retort about spirituality being a private thing.

Next, the mop, bucket and cleaning supplies people. Their strategy is a little different. Their plastic-clad magazines hurtle through your letterbox, only to be forced back out whence they came. The note says that if you don't need any products, they'll come and collect the magazine the following Tuesday, when you are inevitably going to be out. They'll return and return, compounding your unexpected sense of guilt. You're the only one who hasn't returned their magazine and if you don't, the Giant will eat another one of his daughters. Sympathetic? No. We're currently penning a sign to stick on the door inviting their help no more.

Next, the 'just done a local job and have some spare materials, do you want your roof fixing / trees pruning / windows masticked' people. No scary, unhinged individuals in pieced-together old transit vans there, then.

Carpet Man, however, is the exception when it comes to

home visits. Carpet Man is a local Bradford man, by the name of Andrew Walker. He is a man with a mission: to grow his business by providing the best service ever. Now, differentiation in carpet cleaning shouldn't be difficult. From my previous experience simply turning up on time would put most competitors in the well-trodden shag pile detritus.

Andrew's approach is to combine a relentless fascination with understanding all of the hygiene issues related to interior cleanliness and combining this expertise with excellent service to build a loyal customer base.

One of the several tangible aspects of this 'difference' is his regular newsletter. It contains a compendium of articles full of 'secrets for living a healthy, wealthy and happy life'. Cheesy perhaps, but effective nonetheless. He's now a consultant to a range of TV programmes – hopefully our undercover man in the pursuit of getting service wider exposure on television.

I mention Andrew not just because his approach is admirable, but because there's a reassuring reliability in the service. He knows he lives or dies by the quality of service provided. That's a comfort when most of his competitors make Del and Rodney look like professionals.

6

June

'Excuse me. We're holding an event for senior civil servants and aca-demics at the conference centre next door. And as they're as thick as pig sh*t, they might come here by mistake. Just so you're aware.'
Overheard at front desk, West Midlands (really!)

Reginald D Hunter, an entertaining US-based comic who occasionally visits these shores, has the answer to one of the questions I get asked the most. Well, it's the old USA and service chestnut:

Why is service in the US so much better than in the UK?

Reginald puts it so simply, so credibly and so succinctly: it's because American customers are armed.

As the sun breaks through the haze from the chemical fac-tory and the wind carries the smell of the pig farm in a dif-ferent direction, my moment's musing on the impact that arming UK customers would have on service here nudges me into a delicious daydream.

'Here we go,' announces the senior manager to his team. 'We have ring-fenced (insert town name here) to carry out a pilot aimed at improving service. We'll be arming our cus-tomers and observing any subtle difference in the degree of organisational proactivity and personal responsibility and ownership that is generated by this action.'

Here, some wag points out that most of (inserted town name) is already armed, so perhaps they would like to ring-fence somewhere else instead. Others make rude jokes around the words 'ring' and 'fencing', none of which I'm grown-up enough to understand.

Customer at Retail Store: 'You know, I'd use the reward

card more if it allowed you to collect points, like Tesco's Clubcard©, so that you could save them up for something special at Christmas.'

Store employee, noticing bulging anorak pocket: 'Thanks for that. I can appreciate your point of view – and if you'll just give me a moment, I'll copy that thought through to our service improvement team. Now let me take 25% off your purchase here today to thank you for that suggestion.'

Resident to refuse collector: 'You appear to have left behind some cardboard boxes that I wanted removing with the rubbish.'

Refuse collector: 'Thanks for pointing that out, sir. It's my intention to return to collect them when we leave the estate.'

Stressed father outside pub: 'I wondered if it would be OK for me and my kids to sit outside and have a drink and some crisps.'

Barman: 'It's a bit nippy outside, sir, so why not bring them into the family room. We've free snacks, a play area and a video that really works!'

While Americans are now beginning to confront the correlation between proliferation of assault weapons and the number of fatal shootings over there, it may be a little irresponsible to suggest arming customers wholesale. But bear with me.

Yesterday, at one of those 'food courts' in a shopping mall in the Midlands, there was a sweetie stall. One of those where you vainly try to corral your children as they run amok filling up gaudy paper bags with over-priced fizzy cola bottles, strawberry laces, candy necklaces and sharks tasting of watermelon. It's part of an array of food-dispensing outlets, manned by a struggling team. We had something of a wait.

As it happened, a bright and breezy young manager attended to us. I did wonder, however, if a volley of shots into the roof of the building might have galvanised them into a quicker response.

She was obviously used to hold-ups.

Trying to get served at football stadia can also exercise

your powers of restraint. Among the many examples I have received from colleagues is this one. 40 minutes before kick-off, a good friend of mine attempts to visit the lounge beneath the stand where he and his son hold a season ticket. He requires a cola and a coffee. Upon being served by the coffee person (barista would be stretching it given the complete lack of professionalism), after queuing for some time, he asks for the cola and is told he must queue again, at the bar, to procure the soft drink. Once this odyssey is complete, he returns to his seat, with barely five minutes to spare before kickoff. He would have bought a second coffee and some more cola, if the service had been more convenient. Now he sits wondering if there is a link between the lack of imagination applied to service delivery and the current first XI's stuttering performances.

To the untrained eye, queuing, as a concept, is alien to the Spanish. Upon entering the local *pescadería* in the local town, you are met by a crowd of (usually) elderly ladies – an amorphous mob – with no apparent order or process of queuing. However, if one listens carefully, the most recent arrival at the shop will ask, *'¿Quién es la última?'* ('Who's last?'). All she then has to do is wait for the respondent to her question to be served and Roberto is your *tío*.

In England we have some difficulties with the notion of queuing, many of which, I hasten to add, could be resolved through the use of firearms. We are regarded as the archetypal queuing nation and yet are having this fundamental precept eroded by organisations like Tesco who are making queuing a thing of the past. I seem to have more difficulties at Sainsbury's, who are less inclined to regard queues as a problem. I plan to start shouting, 'Who's last?' the next time I'm held up with my half-price asparagus, overheated and queuing. Not sure it would do any good, but it might distract a pensioner long enough for me to barge in.

Whether telephone service would improve as a result of customer firearm provision is, of course, another matter, but it might be possible to send some ultra-high frequencies down the line to the unwanted critical illness policy sales call, James Bond-like. For the manager, coaching the team on service recovery, for instance, would now be based on actual, observable data, like the sound of operators collapsing at their PCs, clutching their ears.

From what we read, the postal service has enough problems without introducing firearms, and emails are increasingly more contagious than the result of a stag night in Bangkok.

OK. Current legislation forces me to concede that I might never get this idea off the ground, but it exposes a gap that someone should be filling. What's the motivation for many people to provide good service?

Let's look at an example of fantastic service and try to explore where the motivation lies.

We're on our way back from an interesting week in Northumberland. For the family, a deserved break in God's own country, surrounded by windswept castle ruins, fantastic local produce, a bracing climate and several hundred crab sandwiches.

Being the adventurous type (I swear I was the first person to wear short-sleeved tee shirts over long-sleeved sweatshirts – albeit through dressing in the dark, rather than sartorial skill), I decide to take a long detour through Rothbury, Hexham and Allendale to Weardale.

Weardale is an often overlooked part of the country, not easily reached by public transport, but once you're there, it offers some glorious escapes. The one we're headed for is Killhope Wheel, once a working Victorian lead mine, now an intriguing working museum, full of activities and experiences and even boasting a small colony of immodest red squirrels.

Parents accustomed to breaking long journeys with young kids might reasonably identify Killhope Wheel as potentially keeping two pairs of young hands occupied for an hour. We left three-and-a-half hours later, vowing to return. And, I hasten to add, I am no geologist. I have no penchant for red squirrels and I do not dream of being submerged in water in a lightless cave for any period of time, no matter how beneficial this is for my children's development.

People make the difference in the greatest businesses and Killhope Wheel is no exception. Our arrival is greeted enthusiastically and our options set out. We can do the lead mine visit now or in an hour's time. If we decide to wait we can do any number of other activities, from processing the output from the mine for lead to visiting the huge powering wheel or taking a walk through the conifers directly over the mine to observe the rare species from a convenient hide.

Our guide to the lead mine is cheerful and knows exactly how to engage the kids. As we approach the 'coffin' – a dark, unlit passage, showing us how the original miners in the mid-19th century would have experienced work – she announces to the kids: 'this is where parents normally get scared, so make sure you hold their hands really tightly.'

To quote Peter Kay, I am shaking like a shitting dog. But my kids assume a knowing attitude, congratulating themselves on their bravery once we emerge at the other side. Nice touch!

As well as bringing some great memories from the mine trip, my daughter brings several litres of water out in her wellies. Again, no problem. The guide suggests that, if we had a change of trousers (which we did), we can leave hers to dry in front of the miners' open fire in the accommodation museum. Subsequent visitors will be surprised to see some pink striped trousers drying on the grate by the waxwork figure of a 19th century miner. Presumably they would occupy the long, cold winter nights by dressing up as Atomic Kitten and singing a medley of their greatest hit.

Having changed my daughter's trousers we dig through recently mined material, to try and expose some lead and, perhaps, to find some fluorspar or other mineral. At this point we encounter a young man as clearly fired up by the subject as my son.

As my kids turn a quiet part of Weardale into the Klondike,

he patiently explains his own fascination with geology, encourages a search for a rare local mineral and cheerfully answers my questions.

From there we visit the hide, whereupon two red squirrels, as if to order, skip around in front of us.

Yes, we'll be back. Yes, we'll recommend the place to others and, when we next go back, we'll probably spend more in the shop. There's added value here – and it's in the feeling that all of the employees, without exception, play out a game plan that results in very happy customers.

It is reminiscent of the story I was told about Singapore Airlines. I understand that at some time their main performance target for cabin crews (hostesses, space waitresses, etc.) is that for every complaint, there should be a compliment. So what happens as a result of this? They cheat. They go out of their way to create compliments. Similarly, at one hotel in South East Asia, you can only say 'no' to a customer with the manager's express permission.

It makes one wonder what performance criteria operate in some of the weary destinations I have visited this year. Only today at my local DIY store (again), late in the day, with no queues, I approached the till with two pots of paint, some brushes, a 13-amp plug and a dustsheet. Something approaching £40 of purchases. 'Hi,' I say as I approach the till. Nothing in return. 'Hi,' again. Still nothing … but, hold on! She stirs.

'Right,' she states to all before her, 'it's three minutes to five and I've had enough. I'm on my way.'

'So am I,' echoes in the back of my mind. I said a few chapters ago that I wouldn't be coming back.

Let's recap. I travel to said DIY store. I hand over £40 and the person serving me appears to see taking my money as a chore. One less chore for her to deal with from now on, I tell myself, and I can say with my hand on my heart that, with the exception of a £8 teak-effect toilet seat, I've not darkened her till again.

But onto brighter things. A Saturday morning in Brighouse

may not sound like a headline to spar with an afternoon in the Maldives, but it provided a few reminders of how positive the results can be when an organisation is designed entirely to deliver excellent service.

On this occasion we're off to visit a good friend: a writer and, to his eternal credit, an editor who was prepared to trudge through all this waffle and proofread it for me. Although he (like me and my girl) is in training for the Great North Run, we decide to take along a couple of bottles of wine and some cheese. In any other town, that might necessitate a trip to the supermarket, but not in Brighouse, for we have 'Czerwik', God's own delicatessen.

'Kids don't normally stay for long,' the proprietor tells me. 'The smell gets to them.'

Not to my two. My five-year-old daughter is sampling some 'Beaufort', a beautifully nutty Gruyère/Cheddar cross from France and my son is nibbling on a sample of 'Mexican Chilli' (you wouldn't). But let's go back to the start.

There's a well-stocked wine cellar downstairs, from which we emerge clutching a Tempranillo/Cabernet from Navarra and a decent Alella from Catalonia. Before we even get to the cheese counter, a young man approaches to take the bottles from us, to put them to one side so we'll have free hands to sample some cheese. The price tickets are peeled off and stuck to the till with military efficiency and we prostrate ourselves before the majesty of Yorkshire's finest cheese emporium.

Now I'm not on close enough terms with the manager to know his name, nor he mine, but you receive the attention of an old friend – the authentic patron, arms crossed, watching over the regulars, like a father to the family at Christmas.

Buying is not a hit-and-miss affair. Ask for advice, try anything, discuss, admire and exchange views, even argue whether the chocolaty aftertaste of the Beaufort is Flake or Galaxy.

•

As my kids agreed on the quality of the Beaufort, the lady

next to me, who had completed her purchases, felt obliged to ask to try it too. Result? Another large portion sold. A happy customer. Some decent banter in the shop. A wonderful atmosphere. We leave £22 lighter. Significantly, my son looks up: 'Dad. They're going in the book, aren't they?'

I'm not going to try to hold Czerwik up as an example to Supermarkets as it's much simpler to provide consistency of good service in a single site operation with the right people. However, for me, it offers a chance for the small independents to fight back. Not only can they support local producers, local tastes and peculiarities, but they can also 'out-serve' their bulkier neighbours.

Vern and Richard, two stalwarts of Halifax market ply their trade (butcher and fishmonger) with warmth and character. Mystified as they often are at claims that supermarket shopping is always cheaper, their ability to recommend, educate, meet your budget and keep you loyal, makes them an increasingly logical choice.

These guys make me misty-eyed, like Rick Stein rhapsodising over a Northumbrian cheese-maker. He knows the value of simple, locally grown, 'cared for' food. I know the value of the service required to build fanatical advocacy and loyalty.

In fact, I promise to streak down Brighouse High Street the day one of the staff at Czerwik treats me like they do at the DIY store.

Weardale, Czerwik, Vern & Richard: all centres of excellence for others to admire and reflect upon.

And on to a branch of Merrie England Coffee House. This particular branch reminds me of an old episode of *Blue Peter*. The one where they attempt to get 16 people into a mini. This place appears to have more staff than you could shake a stick at. But they work like a team, hurrying out bacon sandwiches and hot beef teacakes, fresh orange cups and shakes, 'a coffee and a custard, love'. The same maximisation of space takes place away from the counter, with only a hint of demarcation between smoking and non-smoking areas. Everyone is greeted – and I find myself shouting a 'goodbye' their way when I leave, such is the infectious nature of the place at full tilt. Pretty impressive tray-handling, too. Which also reminds me of an old episode of *Blue Peter*. The one with Precious McKenzie in it. Whatever happened to him? Did he lift up the mini with the 16 people in it?

So what have I learned this month?

My musings over the implications of arming customers have led me to consider some of the best examples of successful organisations, whose eminence has been sown on a fertile ground of individual attention to detail, warmth, knowledge and excellent service. That this is rarely replicated in larger chains is not surprising for all sorts of understandable reasons. But that's no excuse for the lack of motivation I'm finding.

I make a careful note on the nearest piece of paper. 'Must find large chain who provide consistently good service, wherever you use them.'

The piece of paper was torn from the *Guardian*. A few pages further on, Killhope Wheel is awarded top prize for best UK children's outing. It now appears that we're not the only ones to be impressed in Weardale.

7

July

'I'm happy with the company I'm with, thank you.'
> My wife to Electricity Supplier visitor,
> trying to sell us their Gas package

'So you're not interested in saving money. I can't believe you're not interested in saving money.'
> Response from salesman, obviously unaware
> of other drivers of customer service

Garden Centre, West Yorkshire. Thursday afternoon. Not a scheduled visit, but a required errand, given my better half's fanatical interest in gardening. I don't quite get gardening, evidenced by the fact that someone had pinned up a lovely Garden Centre t-shirt by the entrance, but it had been spoiled by two people writing their names across the front. Tommy Walsh and Charlie Dimmock, whoever they are.

We wanted some 4 x 2 brushwood, apparently to screen part of our garden but probably to protect our neighbours from the imminent spectacle of Bradley in shorts: a rare summer visitor with red and white plumage preferring to winter in Spain.

There wasn't any brushwood in stock so we went to the information & customer service point. There we were eventually greeted by a girl who asked what she could do for us. Then the phone rang. She picked it up. 'Hello. Garden Centre. How can I help?'

From what I could make out it was *Yellow Pages* wanting to speak to Accounts. She put them through. Call me selfish, but unless *Yellow Pages* were prepared to make a special journey by car and take their turn in the queue, they should wait.

The situation was rescued, however, by Michael. He came across, explained that a delivery of brushwood was due in today and probably awaiting unloading. 'Shall we come back?' we asked. 'No. I'll get it for you, if you don't mind a little wait.' Great service. Quite literally the extra mile. Faith restored, but some observations to get off my chest.

Frontline employees in the UK are often confronted with processes that constrain their ability to deliver good customer service. Presumably, having the receptionist answer all incoming calls saves the company from employing a main switchboard operator. But it means that any trace of attempted ownership is likely to be overtaken by events, leaving the employee hassled and the customers feeling like some kind of inconvenience.

So why not ask Accounts to take incoming calls? They might learn something interesting about the business's customers and improve their knowledge of the product range. But let's give this place the benefit of the doubt and assume that our receptionist is simply performing the role as an 'overflow'. But in this case, a significantly busier overflow than many of the artificial water features in the yard outside.

Frontline employees are generally prevented from providing excellent service by the way their employers have designed their jobs. In my experience of financial services, those employees who are best at dealing with customers are generally promoted away from the counter, as if the responsibility for dealing with customers is a chore which can be removed through good performance.

In some businesses, personal achievement and peer respect increase the further one distances oneself from customers. I have suspected for some time that European subsidiaries of British banks are simply a 'front' for extreme customer avoidance.

Back at the Garden Centre, there is one receptionist in a circular area. In order to see where customers are she has to be able to swivel her head around nearly 240 degrees. In some businesses, they would sooner see the value of employing an owl than re-designing the space to make it easier for their people to deliver great service.

I see the continued tolerance of these constraints everywhere I go. One supermarket in particular, for example, always manages to have just slightly fewer cashiers than are required to prevent queues building up. This is emphasised by the size of many of their stores, where from 40 or 50 till positions, perhaps only half a dozen are in use during the afternoon. Once you factor in the self-scanning aisle, the 10-items-or-fewer row and the annoyed-service-detective alley (they've got us well segmented), there are only a couple of traditional aisles and they're filled up quickly with tutting shoppers.

Again, it's the frontline employees who have to put up with unhappy shoppers. They are attempting to provide a service within a process that appears to be designed to annoy customers. Whether it's 'Owl' woman at the Garden Centre, 'Pepsi' man at the football stadium or 'Grape' woman at the supermarket, they face constraints all day, every day, that make it impossible for them to give of their best, that place them in situations where, sooner or later, they are going to be on the receiving end of customer anger and that, ultimately, increases their stress levels beyond the point between something enjoyable and a stressful chore.

I recall the times I have been served by an employee in a large chain, who has gone on to tell me how stressed they are and how much they hate their jobs.

Today I receive an email from a friend who has no idea I'm writing this book. She's stressed out, serving hundreds of customers in difficult circumstances without any form of recognition beyond her contracted hours. She's not after free Indian head massages or vouchers to spend at Marks & Spencers. 'Is a "thank you" too much to ask?' she implores me.

Ask yourself, as you read this book, when was the last time you were thanked for a piece of work well done, or for putting your neck out for a customer, for going that extra mile? If it happened in the last week, you're probably working for an excellent organisation. If it happened a month ago, your organisation probably has the best of intentions but ...

If it happened more than a month ago, then your organisation has probably been featured in this book!

Such a simple concept, but so important to people on the front line. Eileen Shapiro, whose book *Fad Surfing in the Boardroom* neatly exposes the frailty of so many 'new' business ideas, attributes business success to the same old basic precepts that have always driven a successful enterprise. If I'm not mistaken, 'look after your people' is the required refrain. From what I can see, it's more a case of 'people getting angry', as The Specials once intoned, in those gloomy Coventry tones.

As I write, I hear on the radio that Towers Perrin, a management consultancy, are publishing research that shows that one in five employees feels 'no engagement' with their company whatsoever. There's even a handy term to describe these people: the 'whatevers'. To prove the point, an interviewer collects some thoughts from the good people of Nottingham, who appear to confirm the contention by describing how, for example, boredom is contained by spending all day on the Internet or talking about the weather.

Our man from the Chartered Institute of Personnel and Development is rolled out to comment. He reckons about 1 in 5 of employees are really stressed out and that in the UK we do not appear to regard employee welfare and engagement as a fundamental driver of business success as much as our European partners do.

Asda is put forward to argue against the point that some jobs, by their nature, are unengaging (divorce solicitor, for example). While you recover from that hilarious line, consider the fact that 91% of the shelf-stackers, cashiers and 'greeters' that work at Asda 'enjoy their work' and 93% feel that they make a difference to Asda's business performance[3].

Does it make a difference? Well, not one week ago, respected researchers TARP produced independent data which showed that from a target segment of 1200 UK supermarket customers, Asda was the preferred shopping destination. 43% of those interviewed proclaimed themselves 'very satisfied' with Asda. The ubiquitous Tesco is second, with, I recall, 37% of customers truly engaged.

Of all the supermarkets covered, Asda was the only one whose customers would not move supermarket, whatever the criteria offered (lower prices, better service).

Fundamental to everything, of course, is service. TARP shows that, from their research, it is the strongest driver of 'very satisfied' ratings. Those of us in the industry know that a 'satisfied' customer is not truly engaged. Those who describe themselves as 'very satisfied' however, are proven to stay loyal, buy more and recommend the organisation much more consistently.

Call me Sherlock, but there appears to be a link between these pieces of information. Asda take employee engagement seriously and produce excellent customer perception scores. So what do organisations like Asda do to engage their people? Let's see.

Several years ago my family went shopping at an Asda in West Yorkshire. Just within the entrance to the store there was an individual, whose job I suspected was to act as 'patron', greet people, pat children on the head and generally demonstrate that Asda wants to look after its customers.

These were early days and the organisation was obviously still trying to determine the right character set to carry out the role effectively. Unfortunately, at this visit, the 'greeter' appeared to have graduated at the Clement Freud School of Extroversion. There were few physiological signs of content-

---

[3] These figures were given on the show based on a recent meeting between CIPD and Asda's MD

ment, approachability, charisma and personality. The man looked depressed. My father, who was with us at the time, had considered walking up to him and saying, 'I'm sorry for your loss.'

Other families, whose children headed in his direction, were equally concerned: 'Don't go near that man! Stay away from him! Michael, get the kids, quick!'

However, to balance out that cheap shot at Asda (and at Asda they're cheaper than everywhere else), I have to take my hat off to them and acknowledge that they have stuck with the role and turned it into, for me, an effective outward symbol of customer care.

We go to Asda and Tesco, for these reasons.

Tesco, while sometimes failing on the personality front, offers reliable service – quickly managed queues, genuinely meeting the challenge to open a new till when 2 or more people are queuing at another one – and, to prove this, is the UK's fastest-growing supermarket, on current data. Asda offers personality, friendly people and, locally, at least appears ahead of the competition on kids' clothing. Not that I wear a lot of kids' clothing.

I like its 'customer suggestion scheme'. If you ring up and make an improvement suggestion, they make a donation to charity for every call. Nice one.

But, on the face of it, the UK fares less well than our European counterparts in service generally.

I recall some research from the Institute of Customer Service some years ago that explored whether people got better service when they were away from home. If my memory serves me as well as Asda does, then it goes something like this. People visiting the UK think the service is worse than in their own country and we tend to think service is better abroad (especially in the US – and we've covered why that is, haven't we?).

Well, it's time to take a short holiday. Let's check this out – and let's do it in some detail.

We fly from East Midlands airport to Barcelona with

BMIBaby. Cheap flights booked on the Internet. It's a good eighty miles to the airport from our house, but the price means that, even including petrol and parking, we're going to enjoy a relatively economical journey.

Several weeks before we are due to fly, I receive an email telling me that there has been an amendment to our schedule. We planned to go for 4 days, flying out Wednesday evening and returning Sunday evening. They tell me they no longer fly to Barcelona on a Wednesday and we have the choice to go on Thursday instead or, if we want, fly from Manchester on the original date.

A bit disappointing, but I suppose it cuts the cost of accommodation in Barcelona!

Being paranoically punctual, we set out on our 90-minute car journey with the intention to allow for a journey of up to 4 hours. Typically, the M1 is clearer than ever before and we arrive several hours ahead of check-in. However, we were wise to do so, because the long stay car park appears to be a month-long trek from the terminal.

We exit our car, pick up our suitcases and observe a solitary, windswept bus stop. Thinking better of it, we begin our hike. I may be exaggerating, but the cost of airport parking is so extortionate, they should carry you to the terminal on a sedan chair and feed you grapes.

The airport is restful, check-in smooth apart from the usual opportunity to watch the English go about their day – one person wanders across to the area where check-in may begin, and everyone else assumes it's about to open and rushes across to form a queue, leaving one Catalan businessman bemused at his seat.

The flight is fine. Attentive flight crew, well behaved kids and a smooth flight, only slightly delayed by heavy traffic in Barcelona.

Barcelona airport is usually in a mid-construction phase; with bright new glass structures popping up like so many crystals to accommodate new terminals to strange and exotic places like Leeds/Bradford.

There is only a slight sense of being processed at this airport and that's at the point where you are waiting for your bags. At some airports it would appear that the handlers are running a book to see who can do it the fastest, with bags miraculously appearing on the conveyor belt minutes before the plane taxis in.

Speaking of taxis, there's a wealth of them waiting to carry you off from El Prat Airport (that's Catalan for 'meadow' before you start making up your own jokes).

The journey is about 13 miles, but can also be made by bus or train. The bus goes about every ten minutes from outside the terminal and is fast and efficient. On this occasion we catch the last one, at around 11.45 in the evening, and we're soon in town to explore service 'Catalan-style'.

This is meaningful for me. Twenty years ago, while spending a study year in Girona, I worked at Bar/Restaurant Roca. This unprepossessing family-run eatery had grown from a small bar to a neighbourhood icon in a few short years. My friendship with Joan, the eldest of the three sons, began then and has endured to this day. From waving him off to do his military service in 1984 to seeing him pick up first one and then a second Michelin star and an array of *grandes premios* for his cuisine, I've proudly watched his progress as he grabbed reins of service and rode his horse into the history books.

Adolescents in Spain see the hotel trade, catering, wine-making and tourism as four grand professions. Joan's tutelage over the years has led me to recognise those elements of service that are equally vital whether you are spending a fiver on a meal or five hundred pounds. Creating a conducive environment for your guests is central to customer persistency. Joan's maybe operating at the 'high art' end of the spectrum, but Brown Sugar, Prêt and Pizza Hut appear to be able to deliver it at the other end. This trip gives me the opportunity to see how widespread this concept is in the country that first turned me on to its possibilities.

Our hotel has been chosen because of its proximity to Bar Heidelberg, a long-established 'German' themed bar /

restaurant on Carrer Universitat. It offers all the required German hamburgers, sauerkraut, frankfurts, bratwurst as well as the full range of Spanish / Catalan cuisine, supplemented by a magnificent range of international beers and the odd *Fleischsalat* kicking about on the bar, for a *tapas*-style nibble.

Previously we've gone without children, but on this occasion we decide to lunch there as a family. Almost immediately you notice the difference from home. Other diners smile as the kids walk in. The waiters immediately make a fuss, find us a table and our particular man makes it his job to entertain our youngest.

My eldest decides that it will be fun to enjoy a game of 'Russian roulette'. Not the one with firearms, but the one they do in Spain with *pimientos de padrón* – a green chilli pepper, nine out of ten of which are mild, with an occasional one capable of blowing steam out of your eyes, Shaggy- and Scooby-style.

Despite the fact that it's clearly a very busy lunchtime period, the service is charming, attentive and, for the kids, what makes this part of the world so special.

It's often commented by visitors to foreign lands that they can dine in a restaurant and then not visit again until some years later. They're then amazed to be recognised and welcomed back upon their return, reminded of facts that only that waiter could have known. It reminds me of the American hotel chain CEO who, apocryphally or not, wanted to match one of his competitors whose CRM system allowed them to recognise customers who had visited the hotel before and be prepared to offer a different welcome for those visiting for the first time.

The story goes that the computer system required to support such an approach was prohibitively expensive, so the plans were abandoned until, one day, the CEO was invited to one of his hotels and asked to sit in the lobby and observe.

The first customer crossing the lobby is greeted. 'Hello, sir. Welcome to (name) hotel! As this is your first visit I wanted to offer you … (etc.).' The CEO, visibly impressed, smiles broadly. The next customer comes in to be greeted by, 'welcome back, sir! It's good to see you again.'

The CEO begins to shuffle excitedly on his seat. How have these guys built the system at nil cost? It's amazing what you can do with a spreadsheet these days! Gotta promote this manager!

Having observed this pattern play itself out over several minutes the CEO is invited over to the front desk where he's taken aback by the lack of any technology whatsoever. It's simply explained to him that when the bellboy greets the customer from the taxi, he asks them if they've been to the hotel before. If they have he raises his thumb covertly towards the front desk. If not, he doesn't.

While you're applying the calamine lotion to this story, it's worth considering whether technology or humans have the greater impact on service. David Jackson turns me on to the improbably-named Lee Tee Wee from the Singapore Management Institute, who says 'humans, as they are more flexible than systems.'

And while you're checking out the relevance of calamine lotion (it was that poor apocryphal earlier in the book) you might be unsurprised to learn that, at a recent presentation, one of my customers commented in the feedback, 'should only attempt humour when natural.' And here's me thinking it was my USP.

Back in Barcelona we visit a number of establishments ranging from the Aquàrium to the Sagrada Família, the Parc Güell and the Nou Camp football stadium. Nowhere do we find excellent service – or at least nothing to write home about. I often do find good service but never feel the urge to pick up a pen and write the word 'home' on a napkin. Is it me?

The *bus turístic* appears to be run by enthusiastic, if scatty, students and the cost (over 50 euros for a tour for a family of four) appears to me, at least, to be a little high.

Being sound arbiters of differentiated service, the kids want to go back to Bar Heidelberg, so we decide to eat there the following night. The same waiter is on duty and he recognises us, finds us a table and spends some time talking to us. My daughter loves him. He tells us he has a 13-year-old daughter and we share some stories.

The best recent one featuring my very own little darling came about when she started singing nonsense songs in the car on a school run. She's 5, so I thought it wise to tell her that if she wanted to make up a song, she needed to find something she felt strongly about. Perhaps the plants and trees, endangered animals, her best friend, helping people less able than herself, for example. She paused and then trilled out the line 'Cheddar Cheese, I love cheddar cheese … I'd like a cow, a lovely cow.' I don't know where she gets it from.

On our final day my daughter insists we go back to Bar Heidelberg to take our leave of her friend. So we go along. He isn't there, but a colleague recognises us as we have our coffee and comes over to chat. Manu, as he's called, has done his back in and can't come to work, but he'll pass on her best wishes. I suspect Bar Heidelberg has created a certain degree of advocacy in my daughter. 'Why are there no nice waiters like that in England?' she asks me.

Spain generally performs well at catering and tourism. For many Spaniards it's a respected, professional career and an oft-chosen path for many students. There are top-quality schools around the country and a well-established path for the best people to follow. Serving people well, in formal or informal situations, is something close to the heart in Iberia, as it is in France and Italy and other Mediterranean countries.

In the UK, in spite of the recent spread of celebrity chefs, the concept of attentive restaurant service appears to be more prevalent in the higher-quality establishments. Yet in Spain, the 6-euro-menu place can be as attentive as Le Manoir Aux Quat' Saisons (not that I've ever been there).

Is there something about serving people well in the UK that smacks of servility? Is there another sentence with more s's in it? The plot thickens, unlike my gravy.

8

August

'*Did you know we do a VISA card?*'

Any bank employee, to me, every day of my life

Today, I access my inbox to discover two great opportunities: 'Visit Scotland' and 'Give your partner more pleasure'. Being a sensitive and creative partner, I opt to combine the two and spend our summer holidays Caledonia-way in a hillside 'hideaway'.

A week in Scotland during the height of the summer holidays naturally provides an opportunity to test the quality of the UK tourist industry – if not the staying power of the entire family.

We prepare assiduously. Anyone taking anything more than a cursory glance at our luggage will know we've been to Scotland before. Anoraks, waterproof trousers, Kendal Mint Cake, shovels, wellies and extra-strength flu tablets expose the family's familiarity with the particular idiosyncrasies of a Scottish break.

Ours is in a small farmhouse just outside Inveraray. Distances in Scotland, like in Australia, are often described in the diminutive. For instance, 'just outside Inveraray' can, at a stretch, mean Oban, nearly a couple of hours away. But on this occasion, it's no more than half an hour's drive across a bumpy track, under the watchful gaze of a buzzard, being swept up the crag side on a warm summer breeze.

Yep, it's warm. Those of you who can recall the summer of 2003 will attest to the scorching conditions. There are Spanish tourists at Loch Ness looking for shade. It hits 32 degrees during the second part of the week. Not what we'd expected.

But how will Scotland score on the customer experience?

Day one involves getting a drink in Inveraray. It's late in the evening by the time we set off with the children and, while the main street is emptying of tourists, one of the local hotels offers respite, at least after I venture in to enquire whether our kids can accompany us. A South African and a German serve us. I make a mental note. Very few Scottish people doing the frontline service roles.

Day two sees us heading north towards Oban. This is a key date for my kids. We're off to Balamory. For the uninitiated, Balamory is a kids' programme revolving around life in a small Scottish island port. It's actually based in Tobermory, which prior to the visit I'd taken to be a Womble.

This involves getting a ferry from Oban to Craignure, on the Isle of Mull, from which you catch a bus up the island to the town itself, whose multicoloured fascias enclose an attractive and bustling harbour. Or at least, to me it does. To my kids, it's the home of Edie McCreadie and Miss Hoolie. It's also steeper than a main course in London. We ascend various parts of the town to access the sundry locations of the programme, take photographs (to share with my daughter's schoolmates) and laugh heartily as father squeaks breathlessly up each and every hill.

After several of these cross-town walks, hunger finally catches us by PC Plum's. Painful indeed. Lunch is bought from a mobile chippie in the middle of the harbour, something we learn to be one of the central attractions in the town. While we screen our fish and chips from a delinquent herring gull, we plan the rest of the day.

First of all, let's get some Balamory souvenirs. First problem. Every family around us has been dragged here by their offspring and – inevitably – souvenirs are required. We search among the shops and finally track down a place with a poster in the window suggesting they may know something. A kid's mug perhaps, a tee shirt, some badges, perhaps a hat – anything to prove we were here. But we are disappointed. Of all the businesses in the town who could benefit from the additional patronage, only two are familiar with the concept of merchandising and they can muster a couple of badges between them.

Maybe the town has been caught out by the rapid acceleration of Balamory into the public consciousness or maybe there is a supply chain hiccup somewhere. Either way, there are missed opportunities. Any entrepreneur worth his or her salt would be salivating over the potential of re-dressing the town during the summer months as an unmissable family destination.

There is a distillery in Tobermory, which combines a small museum. This we visit – and are met by a most engaging host: a warm and charismatic girl who exchanges cheerful observations with my kids. 'Did you know,' she tells them, glancing towards an aloof cat, curled around the bottles in the window, 'he's the distillery cat in Balamory!'

Cue much merriment, culminating in the cat removing himself to the safety of the underside of a Citroen, to consider cashing in on his image rights. Not before a couple of snaps were taken, however, with some delighted children. Proving my own contention about good service, I feel obliged to buy a bottle of malt. For a friend, as you ask.

Tobermory is a delightful place. Well worth a visit. But it could and should do a lot better, especially by following the instincts of the distillery and capitalising on its new 'family-centred' heritage.

Part of the problem is highlighted by a visit to purchase a stamp. This reveals a syndrome that I hear is a regular feature of a visit to some of the more far-flung places in Scotland. It's the 'bored local teenager wants to move to Glasgow, have some fun, turn into Marilyn Manson, but stuck here, so taking it out on the tourists' syndrome. I notice there's now a television programme featuring legions of the disaffected from Campbeltown, highlighting the problem.

It won't be the first time we encounter it on this trip and, in many ways, it adds an entertaining sideshow to our holiday, as we endeavour to find the best 'Kevin the teenager' in shops and, for some curious reason, mainly Post Offices, around Scotland.

We'd lived the dream and stopped off at Glasgow on our way north. Here, and not for the first time this year, we encounter Travel Inn. Not being a man of substance, I prefer to rest in Travel Inns. Apart from the economics, there's the ease of doing business – booking via the web. But, for me, it's the relentless cheerfulness of the people, who, one presumes, work all hours there.

I've observed, throughout this year of discovery, that many of these establishments are resourced by very few people. I imagine some bye-law prevents them from having only one person in their hotels, but my impression is of one or two people managing successfully to combine room maintenance and reception work.

I once stopped at one near Chessington, where I had to ring a bell at reception, late on Sunday evening, presumably to rouse the receptionist. Evidently, she had been sorting something out at the far end of the hotel and responded to the bell by immediately presenting herself at reception and happily processing my arrival.

I asked for some toothpaste but, in my dishevelled state, forgot to collect it. In the time it took for her to return to the far end of the hotel, I emerged from my room to ring the bell again. In her shoes, I would have greeted this with a cuss. She, however, completed her circuit of Chessington with good humour and apologised for not remembering to give it to me on my first visit.

With glowing heart and teeth I retired for the evening. We experience a similar experience on the outskirts of Glasgow. Remarkably, like Chessington, there's a zoo nearby. Perhaps there's a correlation here. The nearer the zoo the better the service?

More likely this consistent level of service is a result of the Travel Inn promise. If you don't get a good night's sleep we will refund your money.

Brave, but apparently effective – and I have seen them

refund money to a disgruntled resident of the Southampton outlet, where a collection of trains had held a midnight party on the line right under his room. Thomas and Percy knocking back the Becks, taking e's, etc., and presumably trying to cop off with Clarabel.

I applaud Travel Inn for having the courage to promote their service standard overtly and, more importantly, to declare the sanction to one and all. Check out businesses across this great land of ours. How many have service standards? Quite a few, huh? How many have sanctions in place for when they fail to deliver? Erm, … Travel Inn. There may be others, but for me Travel Inn deserves some recognition for doing it. Maybe that's at the heart of the motivation in their team. Maybe that's what prevents their best from falling to 'inconsistent'.

The Holiday Inn Express outside Lichfield by the new Midlands Expressway gets my vote, too, simply for responding swiftly to a request for warm milk for the kids one Saturday evening. 'How much?' I ask. 'No charge. My pleasure,' comes the reply.

So back to Scotland. Travel Inn contrasts very favourably with the dreary response to our attempt to find somewhere to dine as a family after 7.30 on a Friday night in the middle of town. There seems to be a paucity of alternatives to McDonalds, KFC and the like. We happen across an enclosed square of restaurants and spy a free table. Italian/Spanish restaurant. Looks good.

A brief chat with one of the waiters reveals that the time has passed by which families must dine. Not aware of this hasty bye-law, we continue our search. Not only is it fruitless, but starter-less, main-course-less, coffee-less and dessert-less too.

Treat-less, we beat a retreat back up the street to Travel Inn. Call me 'The Streets' if you like. Although the adjectives required to describe our frustration would be more likely to occur in an Eminem song.

The family diner attached to the Travel Inn offers succour, albeit it later than anticipated.

The following morning, in the bright sunshine, we discover what a truly attractive city Glasgow is. We find a few places that may have met our requirements last night, but the damage is done. The perceptions created. Let's hope it redeems itself by the next visit.

Back in Inveraray, invigorated by the unusually temperate air, we plan our next outing: a late evening visit to the Inverawe smokery. Again, we are served by northern Europeans, perhaps Danish, not sure. We come to see the bloke smoking out the back. I'm reminded of the time my father once caught me smoking round the back, as a child. To instil a fear of smoking, he made me smoke the whole pack. I wish he'd found me with a woman.

Having had a friend who was conspicuous by her abscess, I feel entitled to throw in the old cliché here. He is conspicuous by his absence. The smokery's closed. Ho-hum. It's late in the day.

Anyway, armed with some smoked eel (they leave no nicotine stains but your fingers stink of fish), we depart.

On a separate visit to Oban we find ourselves in need of refreshment one midweek evening. Our choice of restaurants is governed by our sense of being a family. We choose the one with the widest range of offerings. We choose wrong. I have an intuitive ability to pick the wrong one, which I trace back to my decision to be a lifelong Sunderland AFC supporter. Clearly, about two or three people down, the place creaks, groans and shouts 'I give in' as we negotiate a discount for the appalling service.

Oban does boast what appears to be a decent seafood restaurant behind the mall by the ferry port. Constrained by our budget, we never get to develop the experience beyond the naturally enticing initial perception. Perhaps on a future visit, once the town is rid of its 'bored teenagers' by some enterprising pied piper.

Oban is beautiful, however, and its residents provide us with some richly entertaining anecdotes, especially the two manning the seafood cart, right by the ferries. Here service has led to regular mentions in guidebooks. The refreshing zing of the fresh seafood is only matched by their salty feistiness as we exchange seafood adventures – derring deeds over reckless combinations of *fruits de mer* and vibrant young needle-sharp wines.

This is Scotland at its best. The small, singular enterprises. The dangerous characters. The tasty rogues, imparting their passion and adding colour to the memories.

There's cheekiness, almost recklessness and charisma in these businesses. They are not bordered by rules or regulations. Checklists pall. Passion is unconstrained by convention and one small seafood cart rescues Oban with a winning goal in the third minute of extra time.

Our next outing begins at the crack of dawn. So early, in fact, that the conditions conspiring to create the crack have yet to appear and we sail into the mountains to the ironic trill of Mo Dutta or the measured frivolity of Sarah Kennedy. One of the two. Can't remember. It's too early.

Our mission: to attempt to circumnavigate the Great Glen. I sing 'Wichita Lineman' before the silent bewilderment of the family. They're better at this than me. At a recent visit to a new edifice, they christened it 'Gerald'. Edifice Gerald, anyone?

After descending from a clear, frosty morning into the mist shrouding Glen Coe, our first stop is Fort William. We find a wonderful coffee shop nestled at the far west end of the main street. There are children's activities going on at the back. Unlike Oban, where we only found the best places when it was too late, we seem to have encountered Fort William's service *galáctico*.

There's an encouraging welcome for the kids. There's no evident need to rush the customers in and out, to 'maximise' the retail area. There's an independence of spirit to the place that embeds the experience in your memory. There is nothing spectacular or outstanding, no disaster well recovered or extra mile run for you. But it's clearly prospering and I can recall the experience vividly among a hundred or so hazy recollections.

Elsewhere in Fort William, little is going on, apart from incredulity at the fact that the weather is so good; one can actually see the top of Ben Nevis from the RAF memorial, further northeast of the town.

From Fort William to Fort Augustus and its intriguing array of locks. From there to Drumnadrochit, our main destination. The Nessie experience.

At this point the heat becomes so oppressive that many of us find the prospect of a visit to the Nessie museums more attractive than they should be to a man of average taste and judgement skills. I say 'museums' as there are two of them. Most guidebooks paint a picture of warring hillbillies throwing rocks at each other across no man's land. The reality is rather less striking. We opt for the further away of the two as you head north, which offers a series of video footage exploring the history of the loch, intertwined with some convincing scientific and biological data, adding reality to the experience. Topped off with the ubiquitous Nessie souvenir shop, the experience is a buzz for the kids, but strangely unaffecting for the Mums and Dads.

There's nothing to record. No sense of particular value, but solidly done. I don't want to force conclusions from my day-to-day service adventures. This was akin to filling up with petrol, withdrawing cash or a quick nip to the shop. I wanted it to be more.

This is leading me somewhere. It reminds me of something a colleague tells me. He's increasingly seeing customer feedback that describes 'excellent service' in terms that he regards as 'minimum' expectations. Minimum courtesy provokes a flood of warmth. Have we lowered the public's expectations to this point?

In Scotland, in spite of the glorious weather, we are compiling a list, albeit a short one, of places we will recommend to friends and family. These recommendations carry a burden. You don't want to be associated with somewhere that lets your family down, so you make a few judicious choices.

Among ours will be a visit to the small hut above Inverness, from where you can try to catch a sight of the dolphins and seals and, if you are that way inclined, become a paid-up 'friend of the basking shark'. The young girl on duty that afternoon greets our kids with enthusiasm, rapidly finding ways to direct their excitement towards new concepts and experiences. They peer through the binoculars and scan the Moray Firth. Daddy adds Inverness Caledonian Thistle's ground to the list of stadia visited and several purchases are made and leaflets furrowed away in rucksacks and pockets.

We were the only visitors at that point and the hoped-for dolphins failed to appear, but the welcome, the enthusiasm and the infectious passion of our host remains with us.

Back over the water, we make our long return journey, this time along the southerly side of Loch Ness. Here, according to the guidebook, lies Aleister Crowley's house with all its dark secrets. We give it a wide berth and make it all the way south of Fort William before stopping, roadside, at another fish and chips cart. This time it's a caravan, revealing the intimate site of a small TV among the frying equipment, as our host catches *Coronation Street* out of the corner of her eye.

Again, it's the almost whimsical notion of a fish and chip caravan in the middle of nowhere that begs the attention. The lemon cheesecake and raspberry ripple of Loch Linnhe's glorious sunset accompanies our roadside supper as we trip inland of Oban, back to Loch Fyne, where we find our most pervading experience of the week.

Loch Fyne Seafood and Oyster Bar is perched at the north end of Loch Fyne, as well as in several town centres around the country, from Harrogate to Cambridge. But this is the original location, run by a group of employees so committed, they bought out the organisation and run it, apparently, as a form of co-operative. For my wife, a seafood fanatic, this is the high point of the holiday. The lunch has been booked for several months and a separate budget set aside to leave no shell unopened.

Mussels are off, we discover, but everything else is on. We

detect a northwest England accent in the waiter who serves us and a willingness to chatter and engage as we begin our assault on several courses of the freshest seafood. What led him to settle up here? How can we join him?

My son, a veteran of painful service experiences with his father, who usually remains reticent, feels so confident that he decides to draw a new menu for the restaurant. Armed with crayons, pencils and some paper, he completes his work to the delight of the ladies watching over us. The warm reception his picture receives fills him with pride and, more importantly, removes any thought of misbehaviour throughout the remainder of the meal.

Intrigued as children often are with shells, my two collect and clean a dozen or so oyster shells and wander outside to find some shade from the overbearing heat. Inside, we reach a rapid consensus on the enduring appeal of this place. Shared ownership drives commitment and enthusiasm. Marketing sense too. For within days of returning we'd received our first email from Loch Fyne Oyster Bar promoting their mail order service. Were it not for the fact that we'd spent next month's food budget, we'd be on that phone.

As I write this section, I'm sitting in Club Class on a Virgin train travelling from Birmingham New Street to Wakefield Westgate. Hardly a rock and roll adventure of the scale of Route 66 ('if you go down to Burton on Trent...') but long enough to watch one organisation's approach to service.

UK passengers are largely an inert rabble. We sit, wordless, hiding behind a broadsheet, or trying not to catch the eye of the person whose paper we are cheekily reading. Coastlines may race past the windscreen, but they rarely lift the gaze from the laptop, the patronising mobile phone call or the paperwork. Actually, on a trip through Tamworth a passing coastline might just raise an eyebrow.

We are legion, a brooding mass of low expectations with long to-do lists, little time to complete them and a mental checklist the length of Chile. We want to reach our destination, preferably without being pressured into needless conversation or having a stranger finger our precious newspaper.

One wonders whether Virgin factored this element into their business plan when they successfully bid for the franchise several years ago.

And yet my travels on the cross-country line reveal evidence that the organisation at least has our best interests at heart.

Actually, I don't count myself as a typical traveller. This goes back to my first trip on the London Underground many years ago when I started up conversations with strangers, as I thought I was being courteous. In spite of protesting that I was only trying to be nice, friends explained that such behaviour implied clinical insanity or at least a predilection for following people around parks.

My idea of a great train journey is a DJ playing an XFM-style set, supported by regular wisecracks from the driver ('We're now leaving Birmingham: the drinks are on me') and a decent game of bingo.

Thankfully, someone at Virgin believes that it's their responsibility to inject some warmth and humour into the experience. Today's journey is very smooth, punctual albeit with club class full of mature travellers munching their way through the packed lunches they had to make because they used up all of their money getting a club class ticket. Amid the mastication, the steward attempts to build rapport, in a way that could be described as 'smart cheeky' just as those ridiculous dress conventions are described (smart casual, dirty formal, stained downright rude). Could it be that there's been a concerted effort to maximise the 'human' side to mitigate some of the traditional problems of UK rail travel?

I'm reminded again of the harassed GNER train guard who wandered through the stationary carriages muttering 'I love this bloody job' to an entertained and, for once, engaged throng. As a nation, we're renowned for our left-field humour and yet, when it can really work to make life easier for customers and employees, we hide it away. Because our service conventions tell us too. What a shame.

Today, before setting off, I visit the Café Select bar on the New Street concourse. The conversation is as follows:

'A large latte, please.'

'OK, sir.'

'Oh … and can you make it a strong one, please?'

'3 shots do you, sir?'

'Yes, please.'

'And would you like a cake or sandwich to go with that?'

'Er … no, thank you.'

A pause, while the coffee is prepared.

'There you go, sir. And would you like a cake or sandwich to go with that?'

'Er, no, thank you.'

At this point a colleague of the person serving points out that she's already asked me that question.

'I have to look after this waistline,' I offer innocently.

'So why not have a cake or sandwich,' she replies smiling.

'I might have a cake or a sandwich,' I continue.

'You might want to consider a cake or sandwich, sir, instead.'

'That's fine. I think I'll stick with the cake or sandwich.'

Not a typical, but an enjoyable little exchange, which either proves my point or at least demonstrates the dangers of passive coffee-drinking.

So some organisations, either by luck or design, are beginning to maximise the human factor. Some do it without even knowing. On the way back from Scotland we spotted a 'Taylor's of Harrogate' tea lorry. On the back of the lorry was emblazoned the message:

FOR A TASTE OF YORKSHIRE RING
0800 etc. etc.

Yes, that's right. Not the most helpful punctuation. In fact what is being offered would lead to arrest if it were written on the inside of a toilet door at Chester services. And you thought 'eats, shoots and leaves' was funny.

9

September

'I asked for directions to the self-help section in a bookstore yesterday. The assistant said that if he told me it would defeat the object'
Anon

Today ends with a typical experience. I leave Wolverhampton to drive back to West Yorkshire and decide to fill up with petrol before joining the M6 north. The weather is dull and overcast, like we're all in trouble and are about to be punished.

I pull in to the petrol station, fill up and approach the shop, not even mentally lining up the experience for analysis; it's just a 'distressed' or necessary transaction. In retrospect, I afford myself the expectation of 'transacting' quickly and painlessly, so that I have the fuel to get home.

There are five people in the queue ahead of me, each paying for petrol and only one surly-looking woman serving. I watch as each traveller is processed coldly with a facial expression reminiscent of a prison camp guard, indifference circling in the shop like a wasp with a grudge.

I now spot, to my right, the other server. She's engaged in sandwich re-arrangement, with a level of diligence and attention to detail rarely seen outside of an actuary's tax return. She's not removing sandwiches, but re-ordering them to ensure the ones approaching the sell-by-date are at the front, when we all know that the first, almost instinctive reaction of a shopper is to reach to the back for the freshest one.

Absorbed in her quiet sandwich routine she doesn't see the queue shuffle forward in silent despair. As each new opportunity to raise a smile deserts the main server, I realise it's coming up to my turn soon. Have I the courage to ask her what the problem is? Have I the spirit to mention the fact that we would be happier if the other person was serving? Dare I point out that a smile might not kill her? Actually, on the last point, I dare not, mainly on account of feeling that a recent doctor's visit ended with the strict instruction: and try not to smile, Mrs Misery, your face might crack.

I have not. I have not. I dare not. Desperately ashamed of myself as I cross the forecourt, I wonder whether the company behind the new-style quality sandwich range appreciates the atmosphere in which their goods are being dispensed.

Like the last sandwich on the left, I want to curl up and die. She probably causes more misery than taking the M6 through Cheshire, though, admittedly, she takes considerably less time to dispense her particular brand of gloom.

I wonder about the contractual arrangements between her and her employers. Are they really so desperate for staff that this is the best they can do? It's not as if this is a unique event, a first in a series of thousands of joyous exchanges of money for petrol. This has happened before and it will happen again. The misery wells up like bile in the stomach until one day we read in the local paper of a previously unassuming accountant being arrested over the discovery of a woman beaten to death with an emergency triangle.

As if the M6 isn't bad enough.

So I take a deep breath and wish my mate John was with me. He's the owner of an enviable ability to express his disappointment with service honestly, clearly and, it has been remarked, frankly.

But, as a family going about our day, we often feel like four train spotters who don't know there's a train strike. Oblivious to the fact that no-one is really interested in giving good service and deluding ourselves that organisations have cottoned on to 'service' as a big differentiator, we stoically expect to be impressed.

Very occasionally our optimism is well founded – and I think I've reflected an accurate balance in this book.

However, as often as not, our hopes are dashed on the rocks of indifference.

As part of my job, I often give talks and run workshops on the topic of service. It's a popular subject and the reaction from people to the subject matter is uniformly positive. Most people don't need a business case to understand the power of good service – they know instinctively it's the right thing to do. So, to try to elicit a regular reading of who is doing well, I ask my guests to consider recent experiences and draw up a 'Premier League' of UK organisations. As we dissect the experiences we produce Champions League contenders from the good ones and 'favourites for relegation' for the worst ones.

Remarkably, the trend emerging is for organisations to appear regularly in both lists. In recent months Next, Asda, Thomas Cook and HSBC have drawn extremes of emotions, from 'outstanding' to 'appalling'. One minute one is being praised because of their tangible re-focus on the customer – with greeters at the entrance of each outlet to smile and welcome you. The next minute I hear about the customer who claims he was hounded by their collections department 'every second day' over a misunderstanding. I am, however, encouraged by one of the group, Next, and its September 2004 announcement where they attribute their 30% increase in profits to 'listening to the customer'.

Such experiences (and I cannot vouch for the accuracy of the stories my guests tell) create huge emotional reactions. Someone told me he would conscientiously resist military conscription unless the enemy was BT or NTL, in which case he'd queue for a rifle.

What emerges, time and time again, is a picture at best of inconsistency and at worst, of indifference.

I visit a store in the Midlands during the summer sales. I'm in this shop to purchase some 'night moisturising cream' for my wife and I see that there's a three-for-two offer, so ring her on the mobile to ask her what else she wants (in addition to a moist night).

As I approach the counter, a colleague of the person

serving me is sharing the news with another colleague over the phone, that their store is the top store for sales in the region. But no-one makes any attempt to upsell or cross-sell more products to me. The store is deserted. A characteristic of a top-performing store should be the readiness to say, for example, 'Sir, if your wife likes this product, you might be interested in this one, too, now that it's in the sale'. Or is their success just down to the fact that they are usually in the middle of a big conurbation with a lot of passing trade?

And now a return to Harry Ramsden's. Following an earlier frustrating attempt to divest them of fish via their takeaway section, judiciously edited from this book (it contained a cod-reggae reference which, you have to admit, I was never going to get away with) we decide, nervously, to stop off on the way back from the Yorkshire Dales.

This time, they shine. The regimental dining room, with its echoes of a glimmering Poirot backdrop, sliced bread and tea, reminiscence-drenched conversations and busying waitresses, is at full tilt when we arrive. A waiter, who balances table availability with the priorities of the customers, supervises our wait warmly. He somehow manages to find the nine in our party a table of four and a table of five simultaneously.

From then on, competent service characterised by the odd moment of warmth and personality and an enjoyable meal. Father decides against Harry's Challenge (an immense haddock, whose completion is rewarded with a free dessert) but cannot avoid being drawn to the Spotted Dick, purely for its humorous possibilities ('No, but I've been rubbing some cream on it and it's cleared up nicely.').

Upon reflection, the two experiences we've had here are perhaps understandable. Harry Ramsden's image to me is one of post-war dining, in attractive surroundings, with attentive staff – and 'staff' is exactly the word. It's not a takeaway or yer average fish and chip shop. It's got something special to impart, something unique to offer. Its USP (unique selling proposition) is in danger of being tarnished by these other ventures. And whether these ventures are franchises or part of an expanding organic network, the impact is a dilution of positive perceptions. Just as the previously mentioned pub finds itself in uncertain new territory where it doesn't know whether to welcome families, so Harry Ramsden's has found itself halfway up Whernside without the Kendal Mint Cake.

So, just when your summer duvet is insufficient to head off that first cold snap of autumn and a stew becomes more enticing than a salad, the eating odyssey continues in North Yorkshire.

We meet 'leopard skin shoes' lady in the Loch Fyne Seafood Bar & Grill in Harrogate. 'Leopard skin shoes lady' is expecting a party of five at 1.45 and as we approach the establishment, she welcomes us by our name. A nice touch.

Throughout the stay there are attempts to engage the kids, including taking them to see all of the seafood before it's prepared. She returns to tell us that they were able to name all of the shellfish, including the razor shells, a delicacy back in Catalonia. Surprising to her, but not, alas, to me.

Not five hours earlier I had been invited into my 8-year-old son's bedroom to hear him play the latest song he'd learned on the piano. The tune reminded me of something – a folksy tune, racing up and down the scales. 'So what song's that?' I asked. 'Give the anarchist a cigarette,[4]' he replied. 'Nothing ever burns down by itself, every fire needs a little bit of help,' he murmurs, over the notes. I worry sometimes, I do.

But back to Loch Fyne in Harrogate. It's all of the unexpected extras that make the visit such a good experience. The extras that are missing from most of our day-to-day lives. But does that mean large volume retail business can never differentiate? It's this thought that occupies my mind as my family and I set off, mid-evening, to a local Asda to get some new school clothes for the kids.

[4] Chumbawamba

I'm prepared to note down every aspect of the visit. It's a warm Thursday evening, early September. The petrol station is closed, unexpectedly, and an articulated lorry is trying to extricate itself from the entrance to the forecourt. We park and notice the sign promising that 'if your car won't start, we can help.'

We enter, past the 30 bags of crisps for £3 promotion, and make for the clothes section. Some 30 minutes later we have procured the required items: a pair of trousers, some shirts, socks, a couple of jerseys, a lunch box, a winter coat and some kids' underwear for less than sixty quid. No one goes out of his or her way to help, but we don't need anyone to. The visit is a blur, even in the recent memory as I type this. The checkout lad does his job and we exchange some jokes over the sound the scanner makes, an interesting innovation that sounds like a small animal breaking wind in an echo chamber.

We'll go back because of the cost and relative convenience (and, clearly, the farting scanner).

So, strong, effective service provision doesn't stir the soul. I think we can all agree with that statement. To generate genuine commitment, the organisation has to surprise you with the unexpected extra and/or recover fantastically well from any kind of failure.

As I review what I've written so far I find that these are the stories that have generated most of my impressions of UK customer service, but that's not to say 'adequate service' is bad or unacceptable. Part of Asda's attraction is its convenience and its prices, but that places it on a par with a couple of its competitors, most notably Tesco and Morrisons. Perhaps that explains why we use all three – we've yet to experience the real added extra or the service recovery that would re-route our weekly visits to the one establishment.

It certainly explains why my visits to a certain supermarket are made less frequently and with more trepidation. That decision to brand my wife a shoplifter will take some time to escape my grudging conscience.

I have a coffee with Andy, an old friend in Halifax. He tells me he's just returned from Italy. On his last full day there he found a mosquito net he wanted to buy. Boxed up, he took it to the counter, paid and left. Later that evening, when packing, he thanked his wife for taking the mosquito net out and packing it separately. 'But I haven't touched it,' she replied. They'd bought an empty box.

It was too late to do anything about it as they were leaving the following morning before the shops opened. In passing, they mentioned it to the hotel receptionist who said they'd ring after opening time and see what they could do. Andy left for the airport and, frankly, had consigned the experience to the 'learning' section of his brain (don't buy empty boxes in future).

A day later he receives a call at home from the hotel. 'We've been in touch with the shop and they've said they'll send you a refund or send you the mosquito net.'

Andy chose the net, which arrived a couple of days later. What he wants with a mosquito net in Meltham is anybody's guess, but, as a Sheffield Wednesday supporter, he is congenitally bewildered, so perhaps this is a symptom.

I notice that the consumer page in the *Guardian* is starting to print, initially ironic, but now expressive and warm descriptions of great service, for example: 'I phoned up. A nice, friendly person took the order. I explained a problem with the delivery options. They said, not to worry, they'd be flexible. They were. It arrived. It works. We like it.'

British Airways do this book a great favour in August 2004 by creating havoc at Heathrow by failing to anticipate the number of travellers and also experiencing 'technical problems'. In a quiet news period it makes the front page. Thousands of customers are inconvenienced and hundreds of flights are cancelled. The problem takes several more days to resolve itself and I find myself speaking to the nation on BBC Radio Five Live on the subject of how organisations should respond when things go badly wrong.

There's little time to expound on the theory of the internal service value chain and how it relates to service recovery, but I get the time to offer a couple of acronyms, some personal experiences and to recommend a couple of organisations I feel perform well in the face of complaints.

BA's MD, thankfully, emerges to apologise and explain what went wrong. A few days later BA announce that they are offering all of the employees involved in the problems free flights to compensate them for the stress they were put through. I'm not aware of the arrangements made to compensate the customers, but I imagine BA will address that. What's impressed me is that BA appreciates that if they support their frontline people, that will help address the problem when it next arises.

On the other hand, if I'd had my holiday spoiled by being stuck in a terminal for a day or so, I might not be able to appreciate the contextual efforts BA is making. There needs to be some pain for BA and some recompense for the customer. It takes me back to the Passport Office, their dreadful service a couple of years back and their Charter Mark removal. Customers suffer, reputation plummets, but there's no real penalty, financial or otherwise, for the Passport Office's directors. We all feel hurt, but they go on their merry way, whatever the original root cause of the problem.

Which brings me to Charter Mark. This is a very positive innovation in Public Services that has been around for a decade or more. The intention is to create competition for the award, which must be renewed, and which demonstrates an organisation's commitment to service excellence.

The problem is that it only celebrates the top performers, it doesn't sanction the poor performers – and, frustratingly, it only applies to Public Service organisations.

What we need is a generic service standard, applied by an independent group of 'customers', nationally publicised, containing rewards for the best organisations and their people and containing sanctions for the worst ones. Led by government and perhaps sponsored by a collection of organisations sharing the same philosophy, it would be a concern for all boardrooms and would encourage the reporting of 'service' performance indicators across the land. Organisations treating their own employees badly would be exposed, as would those with enlightened approaches.

Any organisation whose employees proactively ask for feedback? Any organisation whose employees randomly smile, apparently genuinely? Any organisation that keeps its little promises – like, for example, to call you when they say they will? Tell 'em what they won, Dave!

Funny how the ones measuring error rates don't include 'promises not delivered'. Error rate measurement must score some points on a business quality system or, possibly, have something to do with an internal process adherence reward scheme.

If you're in business and you're looking for a reliable, customer-focused supplier, wouldn't it help to have such a 'badge' in place? You've been independently 'shopped' by our fundamentalist service collective and you … were great!

During this month I hear that the Health & Safety Executive are thinking about enforcing publication of results of visits to UK restaurants. Sounds fine to me, especially given some of the post-repast trouser traumas I've experienced in the pursuit of an expanding girth. I wonder how they'll score it. 10/10 – you can eat safely here. 7/10 – standards are OK but we found a dead hamster in the chef's hat. 3/10 – seafood is so fresh we were able to revive the haddock.

So, my frustrated fellow service hunters – will you join me in my quest?

Mine continues, anyhow. A fun experience with a ticket seller at a railway station in the southeast. He'd experienced so many trains clickety-clacking along the track that his tone and speech had come to imitate the hypnotic rhythm. In fact, the delivery of the answer to the question, 'where do we get that train from?' sounded like Lonnie Donegan negotiating the chorus to 'Rock Island Line'.

There's a reassuring rhythm to interactions with people who, by nature of their occupation, have to say the same things time and time and time and time again (point made?).

In September 2004 I am travelling north to Arbroath, the home of the irrepressible Angus College and the 'smokie'. As we leave Darlington a boarding customer asks for a return to Newcastle. The inspector fires off a range of figures before settling on the correct one, as if verbally reproducing his internal computing process: "£52.40 … er, £5.40 … er, £8.40." While the first price does cause some consternation, especially for such a short journey, we get there in the end and the ticket is purchased and I continue Caledonia dreaming.

And like Joan and Ritchie (made-up names), we're 'getting kinda itchy', hunting for a leotard. Forgive me, Mama Cass, but trying to find a leotard for a five-year-old is as desperate and unrewarding as thinking that teenage Russian gymnasts will respond if you write to them (OK, only once and it was a long time ago).

My daughter wants a shiny outfit, pink or purple preferably. I suggest a spotted one (you can tell a good leotard by its spots). I am ignored and the family try to set off from the house without me. Breathless, I catch up and suggest a large sports retailer. As capacious as Jordan's tee shirt, there must be everything in there. They just gotta have 'em.

It's late afternoon, midweek, and we enter the store with its metropolis-style rising footway. You expect to arrive at Canary Wharf, but are greeted by a deserted store. The new Arsenal away strip immediately distracts Father. Not a fan, but a man, so unnaturally fascinated with such garments (I do like the yellow lines). As we enter the bike section, we're approached by a youngster, who recoils as father runs his hand provocatively along a bike wheel and asks, 'leotards?'

'We don't stock 'em.'

Never mind. Never mind that it results in an endless bout of whingeing from my youngest. Never mind that this is the largest store in Christendom. Never mind. They'll know where to get one, then.

'We do get asked a lot, though,' adds the assistant helpfully.

So we approach the main checkout. Father purchases a sweatband. Do I have to explain everything?

'I know' responds the assistant with a Prunella Scales trill, 'we get lots of people asking for leotards, but we don't stock them.'

'Why not?' (Seems a fair question.)

'Dunno.'

'So you probably know where to get one then?'

'Nope.'

At this point, another assistant beams over to us. 'You don't expect us to stock things that people want!' We laugh. It's a brave comment, highlighting the fact that employees have a sense of humour (good) but there's no culture or systems in place to let them influence what the marketing and warehouse people are focusing on back at HQ (bad).

When we finally identify the small store in town that sells them, we mention what has happened at the sports warehouse. 'You should get in touch with them and ask them to mention you when someone asks about leotards,' I helpfully suggest, momentarily forgetting the failure of that toy retailer ever to listen to my helpful feedback. The owner did, but I got the impression the related action was somehow towards the end of her 'to do' list.

Famished, we decide to forego the planned meal at home and take advantage of one of those Pizza Hut family deals. Yep, Pizza Hut is somewhere we go from time to time. It's not a frequency that puts me in the 'super size me' bracket, but it's usually fast, friendly and affordable – and, more significantly, I can't recall any real experiences of poor service.

As the late afternoon sun settles over the Pennines and we agree we've seen the last of summer, we walk in to a bustling restaurant. We're greeted by Sam. She immediately strikes up a rapport with the kids, giving the five-year-old a kids' crayoning pack and audibly musing over whether my eight-year-old would feel too grown up for one.

The kids relax. Not because of the excellent welcome, but because it means Daddy won't be 'going off on one' any time soon.

Out comes the mental notebook. Attentive certainly – the drink refills are all perfectly timed and fairly rapid service – maybe longer than 15 minutes for starters, but that's less of a concern when the individual serving you is spending as much time smiling and engaging with customers as she is in managing the serving process.

I notice one or two other colleagues are taking a similar approach. I see plenty of smiling customers and lots of spontaneous exchanges between team and customers. It's a small diamond in a mountain of rust, but it oozes warmth and paints a picture for me, at least, of a restaurant that must be generating plenty of goodwill, repeat business and, most importantly, the money to justify its existence and future security in the Pizza Hut network.

Contrast this with a national chain hotel in West Yorkshire where I was invited to make a speaking contribution to a financial services conference. The hotel won't thank me for focusing on and drawing the audience's attention to some of the elements I feel passionately about. They won't thank me for one reason. Their service was dreadful. I, fortunately, hadn't spent much time there, but others had and there were many stories of indifference and neglect ranging from dirty coffee cups to being re-directed back and forth for a copy invoice with each team telling the customer to go back to the first team and no one taking ownership.

As yet another member of the audience shared their experiences with me I began to recall what I'd seen on the café menu as I waited in the lobby to make my appearance.

Irresistible combination of espresso, chocolate and steamed milk, lightly dusted with chocolate.

Tempting? An honest description maybe? Fair enough, so why not advertise the service in a similar fashion?

Resistible incompetence and mediocrity delivered consistently by indifferent and plainly hostile staff.

The bank that hosted the conference includes a question on the service from the hotel on their feedback form and, they promise me, they always share the feedback, good or otherwise, with their hosts. After all, a conference is a massive investment, whatever the size. Customer retention must be absolutely critical to the hotel group. It remains to be seen what will happen as a result of the feedback – the unhappy feedback – that will shortly be winging its way to this sad venue.

My experiences to date have led me to mistrust organisations that claim to be customer-focused, principally because of their failure to respond positively to feedback. If managers throughout the business focused on providing perspective and context for frontline activities, then surely there would be a natural interest in getting the customer's opinion, however expressed.

My journey, however, appears to be clarifying the archetypal UK manager as someone far more interested in things other than the customer experience. When I find out what's more important than this, I'll be sure to write to the *Times*.

10

October

'Thanks for pointing that out Mr Bradley. I'll make sure it gets looked into.'
  Employee at Malmaison Hotel, Quayside, Newcastle upon Tyne

No, it's not a joke. It happened this morning. Having booked what I believed to be a family room by Internet a long time ago, I'd received written confirmation of the reservation from the hotel. I wanted to ring up and reserve a table in the restaurant and thought that I'd check to make sure we had the family room safely secured.

'You have a double room booked, sir,' sang the tuneful Tyneside voice.

'Is that a family room? Will the kids fit in?'

'Sorry, sir, it's a double room – just the one bed.'

A brief discussion followed when it was pointed out to me that the Internet booking had actually confirmed a double room, but left '2 adults + 2 kids' displayed in the special requirements column.

I had made a mistake, but one I think that others might also make, genuinely believing they're booking a family room. In the nicest possible way, I suggest that they look at the system as it might lead to some unhappy residents. That's when I got the reply at the top of this chapter.

It shouldn't be remarkable – and if every organisation shouting their customer centricity from every industry magazine article actually practised what they preached and sought and acted upon feedback, then yours truly would have noticed it earlier in the year than October. Only nine months, then.

Creating a 'shop front' that's truly interested in excelling through service is not an easy task and that's possibly why many organisations fail to deliver. The aforementioned perspective needs to be a day-to-day expectation for the people who work there, whether it's Uncle Joe's teapot dispensary or a branch of Boots.

Beyond perspective, there are some basics, like pay and benefits. The old adage that money is less important to people than recognition, feeling valued and experiencing personal development still stands, as far as I can see, except if it does (and most people agree it does) then shouldn't we see frontline people being recognised, valued and developed more often than we do. How many organisations do you know whose main corporate KPI is that everyone's personal development plans are up to date? Me? One actually, but I cheated and came across them while judging a national service award. They are a brewery. Funnily enough, you can tell a lot about an organisation by the things that its senior management prioritise through scorecards and KPIs.

In fact, come the service revolution, we'll expose the great bulk of organisational design as a rickety mechanism to maintain the prosperity of the directors. However badly we perform, there'll be a bonus for us in the end. I congratulate the departing chairman of a certain supermarket for contributing successfully to the company's slide and still finding room in his contract to reward himself the equivalent of a lottery win. In his contract, maybe, but justice?

Some years ago a large electrical retailer would appear to have prioritised 'indifference', such was the anecdotal evidence. Armies of MI teams would be poring over performance on a range of measures from 'impoliteness & discourtesy' to 'incompetence and mediocrity'. In fact when, in 2000, I decided to buy our first home PC, it was clear from the magazines I read that this would be among the last places I should visit. But all of this anecdotal evidence is unfair to them, as I'd never been in any of their stores and, significantly, the data is a few years old.

What I actually did in 2000 was buy a mail order PC from a mail order firm. Back in those days the people writing for computer magazines were recommending Mesh and Evesham Vale as top-notch providers and, while the emphasis was on functionality, price and reliability rather than the customer's experience, they seemed the best places from which to choose.

Performance-wise I was never too happy with my system, but they did replace and repair when promised by the warranty, and although continuous problems led to the machine falling into disuse, I blamed myself for not being a 'techie', rather than the vendor, whom I perhaps should have been blaming, for faulty products.

Four years later and a colleague listens to my sad story and explains that all we need to do is fit a new hard drive. Simple enough, I think and off we go to the once infamous electrical retail.

The branch in my town is very new. It stands proudly opposite my DIY store and shouts, 'look at me, I'm big, shiny and technical.' In days past that would not have turned my head, but not now. Armed with a few phrases learned by rote from my colleague, I stride confidently in several steps ahead of the rest of the family who, from previous experience, have learned to remain close to the main exit.

Lurking in the corridor is a youngster who approaches us and asks if he can help. I explain I need to 'fit a new hard drive', that my machine was bought elsewhere and that I understand it's very easy to fit. I think I managed to keep a straight face throughout as my daughter picks up a graphics card, examines it closely, screws her face into a bewildered crush and tosses it back on the shelf.

He picks up a box and shows it to me. 'That should do it for you.'

I look at the box, give the reassuring nod of a quality manager at a Havana cigar factory (but stop short of sniffing the container), agree decisively with the assistant and march to the checkout. To make conversation I explain just how little I knew about these things, but, at the same time, fearing that someone will come out and surprise me with a television camera.

Back at home I remove the back from the tower case. Mentally, I'm back at the side of my car, sprawling in tears before a flat tyre again. Help me someone. But magically, the current occupier easily comes loose and in no time I click the new hard drive into place and re-connect all the …em, connections.

The family stand back, as confidence deserts me like a bullet from a gun. But, unshaken, I press on, switch the PC on and try to re-install Windows 98. It stubbornly refuses to install itself, preferring to volley a series of incomprehensible prompts, whose common denominator is the word 'failed' or 'unsuccessful'.

Having established that Windows won't reinstall without a boot diskette (just marvel at this technical facility) and having also verified that the boot diskette has left home, I drive back to the store where I'm told they can give me a boot diskette.

Still shimmering with confidence and reassured by the general recognition of the term 'boot diskette' I return and once again fail to stir my machine into a processing frenzy. This time, at the suggestion of the bloke in the store, it's suggested that I ring the help line. 'Not cheap,' he adds, trying to set my expectations, 'but probably the best bet'.

By now you have probably gathered that I was trying to fit an 80 GB disk into a system expecting a 20 GB one. 'Not a problem,' says friendly Teesside Man on the expensive help line. 'But I've got 20 minutes to help you and I'm sure we can get you set up.'

A fine chap indeed, who is able to deal with my naïveté and guide my failing Argos through those big, scary, clashing rocks. He leads me through a number of suggestions that, in the end, take us tantalisingly close to full-on Windows action. Not quite though, as seconds before the end of the conversation, he tells me, 'There's just one thing that could go wrong.'

I won't bore you with the details, but whatever it is, it may require that I perform a 'bios flash'. I once displayed my backside from the school bus window at a group of radiator girls (surely no need of a fuller description here) but I'm sure he means something else.

To complete said manoeuvre I will need to find the motherboard manufacturer's website and download the flash onto a diskette and then re-boot the system with the disk installed. 'Sorry?' I whimper, but these helpline calls are limited to 20 minutes and before he can offer a further word of consolation, the call ends and I sit, head in hands, having been shown paradise and led away from the entrance to Hemel Hempstead instead.

Never mind, I tell myself; I'll ring the helpline again. It's cost me £15 so far – but what's another £5 if it solves my problem?

This time I ask for the first man to help me. 'John?' I squeak hesitatingly.

This time, there's a problem. Once it transpires that I have not bought the PC at his store he tells me he can't help me at all. 'In fact, if I help you, I might lose my job.' Although sympathy is welling up in my heart, my immediate response is to consider, 'If you don't help me, you might lose your life.' That I don't is testimony to the warmth generated by the first assistant. Someone there has my needs at heart, so let's assume Assistant 2 is the renegade robot.

My protests eventually stir a brief response and, hours later, I'm back at the store again trying to locate the manufacturer's website. A little tricky, as the motherboard in question was old enough to have been used to process data relating to the mating habits of the archaeopteryx.

The manager at the store is excellent. He finds the right website and gives me clear instructions, but when I get home I have more problems. I may be a big useless simpering girly man, but you would think this whole process could have been streamlined at some point.

To start with, a few opening questions to establish my

familiarity with PCs might have stopped me buying the first hard drive without first checking the size of the existing one.

In spite of their promise that you don't have to have bought a PC from them to enjoy their helpline support, there is clearly someone on the helpline itself who somehow thinks you do.

There are signs throughout the store proclaiming a new customer focus at the store and a brief chat with the manager appeared to show that there was significant investment in bringing the customer a little closer into view. One sign says that feedback is very welcome as the customer is most important.

I offer some feedback on the performance of Assistant 2 on the hinder line, but apart from a sympathetic grin and a reassuring handshake, I'm again unconvinced that anything will happen.

But the people in the store are enthusiastic and, apart from the first guy whose response to my initial request could have been proactive, they are all friendly and convey their complicated technology in simple terms.

A couple of days later I am speaking to the colleague who suggested that I install a new hard drive. I'm checking to see if he still lives at his usual address as I'm sending round a large hitman to remove his kneecaps. Seriously though, he says to me, 'you know, Mark, PCs are so much better, faster and reliable than 4 years ago, you're probably better off buying a new one and putting it on the never never.'

I curse my trust in everyman, resolve to learn from the situation, take a deep breath and go back to the store and spend £600 on a new system, paying two thirds in cash and putting the remainder on a credit agreement, whereby I have six months to save it all up and pay it off without interest. This is important, as those readers carefree enough to accompany me further into this book will discover.

'Now that the old one shows no sign of ever working again,' I tell the family, 'I think it's time to use my hard earned cash to update our internal hardware.'

The family shrug, as one, and begin to plan what PC games they're going to be buying.

Three days later, at the suggestion of my wife, I ring an old friend, Simon, who takes the old PC, repairs it, restores it to its original condition, updates it to the latest release of Windows and generally performs the sort of heroics normally associated with Dr Christian Barnard.

Relaxing in Coffee Culture in Halifax a few days later, I share the experience with amused colleagues, most of whom privately speculate on how easy it might be to divest further funds from Dork Boy. Now here's a place that provides balm for the bewildered customer service explorer. Coffee Culture was founded in 2000 – making it the first serious example of the new continental café culture in town.

Hidden between a hairdresser and a stockbroker, in an unprepossessing block opposite the oil-tanker-shaped head-quarters of HBOS plc, the team, under the tutelage of Lee, provide a warm backdrop for the pursuit of caffeine.

•

The bar has generated a passionate band of supporters, drawn in from a variety of spheres from the Victoria Theatre down the road to visitors to HBOS and, increasingly, First Direct-style new customers, along on the referral of a friend.

What strikes me about the place is the fact that it is built on a simple, recognisably Mediterranean principle: customers are family and friends.

I recently read about a Scrabble champion who boasts of the 120,000 words he knows. In this bar, the team appear to know the entire population of Calderdale by their first names (second names would be cheating as they're all called Greenwood or Sutcliffe). Not impossible, over four years, but striking in its effectiveness and so reminiscent of those warm Costa Brava holidays where sharply dressed waiters emerge fresh from the *Escuela de Hostelería* to attend to the cheapest order with minimum fuss and maximum warmth.

I focus on the Iberian experience purposely, since the French one is apparently not what it was. Such is the surliness and indifference of café bar serving staff over there, such is the result in terms of falling trade and rising complaints that the main trade association for cafés, bars and hotels, UMIH, has decided to introduce a 'seal of French café quality' which is earned through a positive outcome to 1000s of mystery shopping expeditions a year.

Unlike the Café Place de l'Opéra, which emerges unscathed from the accusations, Coffee Culture has not yet entered the international pantheon of famous cafés. But it will soon, especially since I've witnessed some wonderful service cameos over the past couple of years where the customer has had a problem. If you regard customers as family and friends – and, more importantly, that message has got through to the team – then nothing is impossible and no problem cannot be resolved with aplomb (or even an apple).

The cumulative impact of many visits to Coffee Culture on the customer is the determination never to darken the doors of any of the recent tribe of competitors that has sprung up all over Halifax.

We're practising the sort of loyalty that marketers would kill for. It's possibly also because of the faintly Sicilian ethos of Coffee Culture. I don't want to be found having an espresso in Marks and Spencer and subsequently to have my lifeless and bloated body dragged from the bottom of Ogden Water. I understand that this sort of comment made in jest does not constitute defamation.

But, joking apart, one cannot help be drawn in by the warmth and the blinding clarity of the customer proposition. It directs my thoughts towards other organisations. It's not possible to transfer all of the elements to larger retail organisations, but, again, who's out there trying? What are the elements at play here and how could others learn?

Perspective, I've covered before. Perspective hits you on the head like a hammer every time you go to work for your Mum or Dad, but it's strangely absent from most 'front lines'. We need more Mums and Dads!

Not a claim you hear from many consultants, I accept, but

we need managers to make the context clear, so that informs the way their teams behave. Perhaps we need to look further into customer focus. I'll get my coat.

Flexibility is squeezed out by a combination of over-rigorous, accountant-led systems and the recruitment of people whose prime objective in their induction experience is to learn to operate a till. 'Be nice to customers, mind you' … but not if it means building up a queue. Flexibility and ownership have long been snuffed out in British Retail and I've yet to encounter an organisation that consistently, day in day out, shows me that it's an important part of their business.

In a town like this, most visitors will be working within a few yards of the coffee bar; so one can afford to be flexible when someone's forgotten their money. In a holiday resort, it's a less reliable commitment.

Trust is a necessity for flexibility to flourish, and yet our systems of recruitment, reward and promotion for managers have sown a raging weed of selfism through our businesses that strangles all the dazzling flowers who, stubbornly, through their entrenched humanitarian values, believe in good service.

There must be some out there, though, and it's with this thought that I pay a visit to Carphone Warehouse. My colleague John tells me in his frank and engaging style (and he's heard the PC store story so he offers advice of this nature very tentatively) 'the hands-free system in your car is rubbish. I can't hear you. Get yourself down to a phone shop and get a "beat the ban" kit.'

I choose Carphone Warehouse because that's where I first went to procure a mobile phone. It was one of those blue Ericsson models that looked like a marital aid. Designed for action, the purchase of said phone also gave you a free mountain bike. A combination too exciting to resist. As you ask, the bike was sold before I used it.

Anyway, Carphone Warehouse has some strong principles around independent advice and value. Those of us aware of such things note a huge gap in customer perceptions ratings between these boys and their nearest rivals.

I visit a store in a nearby shopping mall, initially to enquire about the 'hands-free' pack. 30 minutes later I emerge with a new free phone, complete with photos, video, voice recording, bluetooth, vegetarian options, wide screen, low fat, washing and drying cycle, microwave and combination grill, extra stretch lycra with buttons on.

It turns out I had amassed quite a sum of calls to earn myself such an upgrade, but it prompts me to ask about how they ensure people aren't pushed towards the costlier tariffs. The fact is, I discover, the frontline people receive the same level of sales commission whatever the tariff, so the focus is on the quality of advice and service and not the sales push.

I am later told that all managers throughout the business are bonused on service and quality. I haven't verified that fact independently, but it strikes me that we've found one organisation whose success is rooted in the principle of providing 'Dads' near the teams on the front line who are creating the right environment for those people to sell.

Or is it Mums? There's plenty of evidence to show that working environments led by women are more engaging, supportive and inspirational than the traditional set-up.

During my visit I show interest in a new service, but don't have the time to sort it out on the spot so I agree to receive a call later in the week. It doesn't come (although I've forgotten and am not expecting it). However, the following Saturday I receive a call apologising that they haven't been in touch and that another call will be made the following week. That's a while ago now and they still haven't called. So nobody's perfect, eh?

Nevertheless, considerably more engaged in the company's ethos, I go to see Charles Dunstone speak at a Customer Service conference. He founded the company, famously out of a garage in London. Instinct would appear to drive his decisions – his approach seemed more to be around instinctively seeing customers at the centre of the business and then asking himself: if we were serious about this, what would we change?

So, amid the gloom of UK service in the 00s, there are a few shining examples of good service. What appears to unite them is a self-effacing attitude, an admission of learning not yet achieving, and a fundamental belief in the business case that links this focus to the bottom line.

Anyone who believes in customer service is armed with a mountain of persuasive case studies showing that good service ultimately generates cash. However you measure it (and one way is to ask your people regularly when they were last thanked for a piece of work well done – then compare density of 'thank yous' with bottom line figures, and I swear on my auntie's gallstone you'll see a correlation), it's proven.

The happier your employees, the happier your customers, the more productive your business, the better your results, whether you sell coffee in Halifax or provide the telecommunications structure for the UK.

In fact, as there are no businesses where the customer's loyalty is guaranteed, shouldn't everyone be doing this? Wait a minute, no businesses where the customer's loyalty is guaranteed? I seem to have overlooked one particularly pure example: association football.

October 2003 and we arrive en masse at the Stadium of Light to see Sunderland hopefully toy with Reading, like an adolescent tom cat, before dispatching them ruthlessly. See, the language has started, I'm getting fired up, there's no rhyme or reason for it … would you look at Julio Arca's side-shuffle, shouldn't he be sainted?

Sunderland, Huddersfield, Halifax Town, Bradford City, Leeds United – one the closest to my heart and the other four the closest to my house. My pal Dave knows a lot about customer loyalty, he's doing a masters on the subject – and yet, famously, he rubbished the link between satisfaction and loyalty by confirming that he still went to see Huddersfield Town play every Saturday, in spite of the level of service delivered on the pitch. Not much satisfaction there. End of story[5].

Football generates loyalty like no other entity. And it bears some scrutiny. I believe it offers a real insight into why some organisations are more successful than others, and my many travels have thrown up a compelling and persuasive case.

Fans 'love' their clubs. And it's a 'love' like the greatest love a long-term partnership can share, punctuated by periods of despondency, argument and joy, but underpinned by commitment, understanding and passion; a need to grow old together and pass the baton down the generations.

I became a follower of my team out of sympathy for my father, when, shortly before my 7th birthday in October 1969, he and my Uncle Ken took me to see Sunderland and Chelsea share no goals, three passes forward and several thousand in the opposite direction. Amid the gloom of the return journey, I must have sensed what it meant for my father, since my mother confirms that I told her I was, from then on, in sympathy with him, a Sunderland supporter.

Do you fall into using a particular brand of toothpaste as a result of sympathy with your father? Probably not, if the tooth were told. So relationships between clubs and fans defy an immediate logic. It could be the colour of the strip, witnessing a great match, just as much as being a result of where you were born.

But it generates a loyalty that seldom exists elsewhere. My mate Kev once ordered the Lisbon Lions commemorative vintage shirt from his beloved Celtic via their Internet store. What arrived was a vintage shirt from another period, maybe the Feyenoord match. So, did he return it angrily, demanding a refund? No. He thought, 'I like this too. I'll have both,' and got on the phone to sort it out.

Football Aid, for me the one organisation that has under-

---

[5] Since writing this hilarious observation, Huddersfield Town have experienced a renaissance and are currently challenging for a return to the Coca Cola Championship.

stood how to maximise this passion, offers fans a chance to bid to play on their favourite club's pitch, using the funds raised to help the fight against juvenile diabetes and support a variety of club charity causes. One only has to witness the expressions on the faces of the fans as they walk onto the hallowed turf to understand what it means. I do it in 2004 and, among the many wonderful memories, are the words I hear from the tall, imposing figure behind me, as we walk the steps down to the home dressing room and a meeting with two of our heroes: 'I'm so excited I could wet myself.'

The only possible analogy with UK service in general would be that, on occasions, I've waited for a train for longer than men's bladders were designed to hold water, but it illustrates the point. Football's passion is beyond the reach of UK retail, but it does offer a few pointers.

Firstly, true loyalty is not bought through inducement, through special offers, be they extras, more of, or price reductions. There's a second, more profound level of loyalty enjoyed by football clubs, but which many businesses could strive for, if they realised it was down to the level of emotional attachment.

For this insight (and many others) I'm indebted to David Jackson, one of the UK's brightest and most engaging thinkers on organisational design. Money may persuade me in to the deal, but the real leverage only occurs when we're emotionally attached to each other. I see this happening with companies such as **www.amazon.co.uk** whose technology can reproduce the nuances of a strong relationship: they know what I like and make sensible recommendations. Although I am increasingly tempted to throw them a curveball and start to take an unnatural interest in books on Mexican anthropocosmic theatre.

Again the failure of organisations to understand where customers' emotions are generated inevitably means that the rewards will continue to elude them. These 'misery' shopping experiences, as a colleague once described them, are plainly showing that few organisations have made this connection. As the great Canadian stand-up comic Stewart Francis once said, many of the employees look so frustrated, that it appears their previous role was as a price-checker in a Pound Store. ('How much is this? A POUND!') Those that have, admittedly very few, have made me a 'fan' – and I use the word advisedly: they have generated a real emotional connection and I find myself talking with pride about them.

The majority of my day-to-day experiences – a series of murmured monologues, face-down, lifeless and indifferent – reveal the breadth of the ravine between current perform-ance and every company's aspirations. The gap is under-standable, but the failure to address it is unforgivable.

I visit HMV in Leeds to buy a PC game for my son. Music, as Madonna says, brings the people together, so perhaps this is an industry within touching distance of football. In addition to my purchase I have a query about an obscure salsa artist named Juan Luis Guerra. Do they stock his new album? It's been out a week or so in his native Dominican Republic.

The man who serves me resembles some kind of Scandinavian messiah, long blonde hair, beard, a kind of Bjorn Borg the Baptist and reminiscent of a character we used to meet in a pub in Sheffield when we were at University. I recall him being allocated the name Jesus of Gothenburg. To me, this looks a real music man. Someone who appreciates the passion and emotional investment one makes in one's favourite music. No they don't stock it, but I should check out **www.hmv.co.uk** since their import titles are all held in the big store on Oxford Street and that's where the web store gets them.

Good advice and something to bear in mind for the future. I check out the website but the title retails at a good £6 more than on Amazon, so that's where I'll be going. Well, er … that's where I do go, but they can't get hold of it quickly enough, so I go to **www.amazon.com**, from where it costs the same as in HMV if you include the postage from America. What goes around comes around.

HMV does, on the other hand, knock spots off most of its competitors when it comes to sales and a friend, who buys up to 20 CDs at a time there, is certainly keeping their bottom line healthy.

So in football our passion for the Club generally exceeds passion for the players, with one or two exceptions, but with music the artists are far more important than the brand selling them. So how could the music retail business develop the emotional connection?

I always remember where I bought a CD and the recollections range from second-hand stores in Sheffield to the Corte Inglés website. But in general terms, and this is borne out by my journey, the people are employed as checkout operators, so, other than the final transaction after much browsing, there is little opportunity for interaction with the people there.

At HMV I have experienced a couple of occasions this year when employees have approached me and asked if I needed any help. Promising and indicative that a change in retail music selling may be impending.

But what would the ultimate vision be? I dream of a store where there are two or three specialists within the browsing section, sat at desks, able to source information for you and introduce you to new styles and different genres. At busy times they would double as checkout people, but their roles would be to ask people if they like the music being played. Is that what we would normally listen to? How often do you buy when you browse? How could we make the experience better for you? What sort of offers would make you hand over more cash? Yep, I'm back on the asking for feedback trail – pointless though it may be.

A good long chat with a vibrant, infectious music fan might just prevent the anticipated decline of CD sales and offer a richly rewarding alternative to downloading.

It's possible that the increased cost of providing such a service could be added to the CDs themselves. Or is that why Andy's Records closed? Those guys knew what they were talking about. I hope that people weren't taking their advice and buying the CD for a tenner at the supermarket.

A richly rewarding alternative to having to go to the bank, the dentist or the petrol station would also be welcome, but unlikely. These are what are sometimes called 'distressed' transactions: the sort of things we have to do – the basic hygiene activities of our frenzied dance on the planet.

They don't come any more distressed than a visit to the dentist and mine, one Mr Azam and his associates, do take pleasure in making a connection, especially with kids, switching the focus from how much it hurts to how proud you must feel, reminding me of the 'Killhope Wheel' coffin and those scaredy-cat parents.

It's rare there's any emotion in the ATM and refuelling transaction – and it would be foolish to believe there's an expectation of much more than simply transaction fulfilment. In fact, my travels highlight the glumness of such experiences, whether it be in the growing queues before the diminishing numbers of tills at your bank or spinning your coin raffishly into the receptacle at the M6 tollbooth.

And while you can make the case for an occasional smile on the face of the person serving you, I'm not going to press for maximum joy all day.

However, in other transactions, joy … well, maybe an apparently happy demeanour, can make all the difference.

Take my new pal (as Keith Floyd used to say) Gearoid. I break my return journey from Arbroath to carry out an errand in Edinburgh. I feel the first faint stirrings of the requirement for an emotional transaction. I'm hungry, it's the rush hour and I find myself spinning around in Waverley concourse amidst the Costas, Delice de Frances, Bagel Factories, etc.

Being a man of some culture and displaying a taste for the healthier things in life, I opt for the bagel. 'In fact, I sometimes don't even charge people.' I catch a few words. What?

Our man is extravagantly engaged with a customer and clearly I have arrived at a key moment. 'And you know what?'

he continues, making Graham Norton look decidedly intro-verted, 'he's my boss and he lets me' – he smiles at his col-league.

Evidently there's some Mickey-taking here. Clearly all the customers are being charged correctly. But a different prod-uct altogether is being cooked up here.

'I love customers,' he tells me as I approach the counter. 'This is the best job I've ever had. I get to talk to people and I love it when they make me laugh. That's what I was just say-ing – if you make me smile, I won't charge you!' The man deserves a medal.

He fixes up my bran bagel, toasts it, has time to take a call on the mobile and several other customers and I join in. 'So you're a call centre too?' 'Better than any one I've called.' 'Now do you want some tea?'

There's a giddiness to the experience. Late October and I finally find the service messiah, unexpectedly operating as a bagel dispenser in Edinburgh.

What is first an orderly queue, displaying all the restrain of the British, is now breathing, talking, exchanging jokes. 'Put it on castors and you could clean up,' someone offers, point-ing at the small cabin that encloses him. A few customers could push his operation up the ramp to Princes Street and do roaring business amongst the bagpipe-players and the American tourists.

I wonder if this has been staged on my behalf. I wonder if someone slipped me the lysergic when I left Arbroath. Maybe the experiences have got the better of me and I'm hallucinat-ing. I'm not. Gearoid not only displays the famed wit and warmth of the Irish, but he's putting it to miraculous effect. Both myself and the customer behind me reward him with tips approaching 100% of the transaction value.

I find myself telling him about my book. I tell him he's the last-minute winner, snatching victory from the jaws of defeat. I'm so exhilarated by the experience that I buy a healthy seed and fruit bar that I end up disposing of a little later.

This man could probably fulfil his promise of not charging the odd customer and still guarantee Bagel Factory's future prosperity. I ask him to write his name down for me.

This is one of the very few examples I've seen from the far end of the service spectrum. There have been experiences, admittedly few and far between, of an individual or an organisation improvising a great recovery when things have gone wrong or wonderful flexibility in the face of an awkward request. These are the everyday opportunities that present themselves to organisations. What even fewer do is try to inject a little of the unexpected into the everyday transaction, so that the customer is taken aback and never forgets.

As I write, the Virgin Trains boys pass down the corridor with the surveys. 'You could win a year's free travel if you fill in one of these,' they tell the passengers. They don't give me one. Has someone fingered me?

II

November

'I'm afraid we don't have enough people to man our automated barriers.'

Unlikely explanation issued to a friend who's annoyed that only two of several motorway toll booths are open and the ones allowing him access with his 'tag' are all closed.

(November 2004)

I have previously acknowledged that many customers of organisations, like certain football fans, bring a number of other challenges to the front line, in addition to their passion. The front line at WH Smith at King's Cross, as I have written, displays tremendous courtesy and fortitude before many of the rudest people I have ever encountered (a significant minority in a usually orderly crowd).

Working on the front line in the travel industry in general, because of some of its infrastructure and quality issues, cannot be an endless daisy chain of joy. I smile nervously, chew up inside and wait when there's a problem, but some less introverted customers take it out on the staff.

So if we fail to acknowledge this endemic symptom of service failure, we fail to protect our people and we generate a tide of dissent, an emerging readiness to fight fire with fire and to fight back.

I read that 43% of retail employees have, at some stage of their careers, been the victims of an assault by a customer. I see the perpetrators everywhere I go, taking out their inadequacies on people on the front line. Perpetrators who, according to an eastern philosopher, would be 'immeasurably improved by death'.

It doesn't matter how well you tell your people you appreciate them: if you leave them unprotected, they will not repay you with outstanding service. The abuse I see doled out to the team at WH Smith in King's Cross by some fat, chalky-faced city mutant would provoke me, even me, into violence. We have to protect our people, especially in stress-inducing industries like travel and football.

'We don't have any words for people who abuse our staff,' say GNER's posters along the length of the east coast line, 'but here are some sentences.' The notice goes on to describe jail sentences for threatening behaviour, actual assault and verbal/racist abuse.

And yet, when it happens, we slink away. When the low life swearing at the ticket-seller at Wakefield Station, who's only trying to explain why a train has been delayed, finishes his ugly tirade, we cough, divert our eyes and smile apologetically.

I can't imagine there are many UK organisations that have not alighted upon the strength of the link between happy employees and happy customers. As a general retail precept, it's writ large in the training book, but if it is so clearly proven, why do so many organisations feel it is acceptable to leave their frontline employees exposed and unsupported?

Why does an organisation feel that an abused member of staff will provide consistently excellent levels of service?

Having said that, some of these organisations aren't actually asking their customers what they think. As obvious as it sounds, there are few informal, conducive or pleasurable ways to provide feedback to organisations. So, why don't these organisations ask us what we think?

They do, of course, I hear you cry ... but do they? Really?

They may send surveys out to us from time to time or, like the guys on the Virgin train, they may hand them out for completion. But what happens with that information? If, for example, you use the form to explain that the lack of a smoking compartment in first class is unacceptable, how do you know this will be acted upon? What makes you, the poor consumer, believe that your comment will somehow rise above the statistical significance level and appear like a burning light-bulb of inspiration in some distant market research department? How many organisations could honestly respond to a single customer's individual comment positively?

A nice start would be to provide us customers with the results of their surveys in the first place. Instead of my getting a call from the outbound agency employed by one retailer to sell their cash-back health plan to me (as has happened today, as I write this), for which, incidentally, I have no need whatsoever, why don't they email me the results of their last customer survey?

But the reality is that customer research sits proudly under the ethos of market researchers, whose brief and passion is the science of understanding the greater trend. Laudable though that might be, especially in the pursuit of new products and services, it does not address the service gaps I am finding on this sad pilgrimage.

I have struck up several conversations with lovely people, doing their best in a number of organisations, who tell me, without seeing the futility of it all, that they don't get to participate in deciding what questions their companies should be asking customers. They don't get told that the survey has gone out, so when a customer mentions it, they can't answer any questions on it. They don't get to see much of the results, if any. That information tends to disappear into management meetings, to be chewed on for weeks and eventually, as my pal David points out, to be converted into improvement instructions and imposed thoughtlessly on the people on the front line.

But isn't the whole point to create an environment where your customers are entitled to receive consistently good service. If your own people aren't even trusted to take part in the feedback and improvement process, what chance have you got?

My journeys are revealing very few organisations whose

people find it part of their jobs to ask routinely for feedback. I poke fun at the toy retailer, but they are not alone. For the last four trips to my local petrol station I have asked for first class stamps and they have only offered second class. Now true proactivity would be for them to advise me not to use the mail at all, it's far too unreliable. But it would have been nice if the person serving me had said 'you're not too lucky with these stamps. I'll see if I can get more in.' You're more likely to get the response I get at the out-of-town sports store ('As if we'd stock something the customers would want').

If we did that, we'd find that most of us out here, being buffered between the mobile-phone-offer sandwich-boards, have some basic requirements – and they're not always the ones you might suspect we have.

I've covered ownership earlier in the book, but I think it's the key. When the coffee isn't paid for because they saw how long I had to wait, I feel good on two levels. They've sorted me out, nice one. But, secondly, I make assumptions about the sort of company they work for. Good ones. I might come back – and I'll certainly tell a lot of people about it.

The thing about ownership is that it applies to any business. You can't offer a 'cop out' card if you work on the railways or in public office. Each time we thrash our way through the bracken of email, phone and post and encounter a human, their ownership can make or break your relationship with that organisation.

Where I have seen ownership, it's almost always been a place where I've seen day-by-day team gatherings at the start or the end of the day. Presumably the boss is giving people a bit of perspective on what's going on, where the business needs to focus, what we have to concentrate on today, where we went wrong today and, you'd hope, what you think we could do differently today. Prêt and Asda, from what I've seen, appear to believe in this, even if its deployment isn't always consistent.

Ownership has been conspicuous by its alarming scarcity in UK retail. Misguided emphasis at contact centres constrains the endless possibilities of the human interaction and downcast shop assistants and checkout operators eye the queue more than the relationship.

While the quality and nuance of the human interaction comes sharply into focus as the key differentiator for most businesses, our contact centres relocate to India 'to improve service'. My complaint is not that the folk over there are unable to provide good service; it's just that a perfect telephone interaction contains a sub-text of several conversational elements (for which I'm indebted to James Eagle and Guy Fielding), which it takes a native to understand fully.

If the argument is that they're simply there to take a call and give some information, then why not have a machine instead?

Machines are great, wonderful, reliable, steely-charactered things. At an NCP car park, for example, obtaining your ticket and, upon returning, inserting it to make payment and departing smoothly, has become the general expectation. Unless, of course, two thousand of you have just attended a Finn Brothers concert in Bradford and are all trying to process tickets in the machine at the same time, 10.30pm, forming a queue that goes around the block twice and which would place some pressure on all but the most incredibly compliant baby-sitting arrangements.

As I have said before, humans are adaptable and machines aren't.

There's nothing new in these insights, just as there is nothing new in the basic bonds that bind us in our relationships: trust, support, empathy. The latter most usually begins with a smile and is followed up by picking up on a conversational hook, if appropriate, and making the customer feel valued.

The team at WH Smith at King's Cross usually have unfeasibly large bars of chocolate to offer you at half price when you purchase a particular magazine ('Would you like this two kilo bar of fruit and nut with your *Men's Health* magazine, sir?') but, as often as not, it acts as a hook to raise a smile and make the thirty seconds you share anything but a chore.

So, we are herded like sheep on to trains and we detach our brains along with our walkmans. The poor guy serving tea and sandwiches from the trolley on the train slowly moves down the corridor. The people in his way, wanting to pass, appear to have failed to spot the option of standing by an unoccupied seat, so that the man can pass by and do his job. I have no idea how good the service on the new *pendolino* will be, but I do not expect the employees to be able to levitate their snack trolleys. There, that's not a phrase you hear every day.

Yet, as employees, we are a powerful force, full of imagination, perspective, practicality and passion. We understand the weak links in our company's strategy. We see the loopholes in the process, we know the strength of the proposition, its limits and we know how to put it right. But we only share this with our colleagues.

Again, on a train journey, I catch a conversation opposite. A group of railway workers are off to a conference and are discussing the state of the business. 'It's definitely going to happen,' one of them mimics a senior manager. 'He said it's about 10% certain.' Laughter breaks out.

They debate IT resources, people distribution and policy. They pick up on opportunities and sensibly debate the issues, pros and cons, figuring solutions that fit the context. I may be wrong, but I'd be surprised if any of this is shared with the bosses.

I sip at my tea. It's hot. As I drink, the tea appears to be seeping back out through my brow in the form of sweat. I look like a surreal recreation of Diana's memorial fountain, dripping forehead and plastic cup. 'They wouldn't let kids play on me,' I muse. But I note down some broad conclusions.

Everyone wants to do a good job. Everyone wants to play a part. Yet we design these businesses to reward the leaders for creating the environments that constrain the imagination and leave creativity in a siding near Thirsk. Is this another symptom of the grand service malaise that I'm uncovering?

I recall the tub-thumping speeches of former chief executives, blaring vision, values and beliefs from the gaudy platform at the NEC. Our strategy, blah blah blah. Your part in its achievement blah blah blah. Share my vision? Probably not, unlikely as that may seem.

The detail disappears into the air like a feeble cadenza – unformed and nebulous. Like Field Marshal Haig, he'll misinterpret the great Chinese general who said that 'great leaders walk behind their people'. In Haig's case, he simply overestimated the distance.

Like so much icing on a chocolate cake, the seagulls settle on a newly ploughed field, and I conclude that few organisations have rigged it so their people feel good – and perform accordingly.

I reflect on the subject matter. Complaints, by their nature, represent a challenge. No process can be written to replace the flexibility of human intervention. That's because complaints can be addressed in so many different ways. What's one customer's compensation is another's warmly expressed apology. The line is blurred and some vibration around the baseline is natural. It does not fit systems; it requires art over science, human intervention over logic and policy.

When you do reflect on this blurred line, you recognise the importance of flexibility in the process, be it an absence of average handling time measures or the simple instruction to 'use your best judgement at all times'. Presiding over such anarchy preys on the minds of our executives and they resist creating the right environment, preferring what they see as predictable and reassuring order over freedom and chaos.

So we've begun to share the blame for the current predicament. Unengaged employees, not blessed with the appropriate skills, feeble customers not brave enough to intervene, not interested in complaining, and managers happy to lap up the adulation of the annual bonus, in no way representative of the true driver of success.

I wander into a branch of Prêt at 8.30am one chilly November morning and order three lattes and a cappuccino. My man takes the order and his colleague smiles from behind, checks it back and starts to operate the expresso machine. At this point my man removes himself to the side of the bar to replenish the stock of cup carriers. In the ten to fifteen seconds he is gone the customer behind me mutters to himself, throws down a pound coin and leaves with his two bananas. 'He didn't seem very happy,' a lady pipes up, 'he was swearing under his breath when he left.'

Now call me the caped customer service crusader (oh, go on, please), but such a lack of forgiveness is surely unreasonable. Fair enough, whoever checks the cup carrier supply needs his bottom smacking soundly, but a fifteen-second delay is hardly a huge service failing.

But this is London. Life is faster than a very fast, speedy, rapid sort of thing and life here is unforgiving. Customers of a large, national building society chain score its branches low on service in the southeast, but, curiously, score them higher in the north. Is there a cultural variance at play here?

Smiles are extracted from customers like teeth in the City and playful contributions from yours truly are either ignored, met with a sort of aggressive indifference or treated as unnecessary decorations. It's not Christmas yet.

I check in to a Travel Inn hotel later in the evening. There is a group of customers being checked in, in turn, and there is an air of calm, very soothing to a tired visitor.

I like Travel Inn for a number of reasons, largely a combination of cost, convenience and a general commitment to service, predominantly through the promise that if you don't get a good night's sleep you don't have to pay.

On this occasion the last person before me is a woman. The young lady processes the transaction and then explains that, as the guest is a woman and in single-room accommodation, she will be writing the room number on the invoice rather than revealing it to all and sundry. I look around to see who poses the immediate threat, realise I'm alone in the lobby, smile nervously and approach the counter. Though I'm tempted to ask for the room numbers of all single females, I genuinely applaud the approach and tell them so.

I don't for one minute believe that Travel Inn is the only hotel to employ this policy, but the fact that it is actively deployed, like the good night's sleep promise, impresses this weary traveller.

Some thirty minutes later, my three colleagues arrive at their hotel and experience a different level of service. My woman has nipped off for supper and one young man is coping with a large queue. To make matters worse, my colleagues spot a head briefly appearing at the office door. It spins around, computes the situation and disappears as rapidly as it appeared.

It could be the manager at the card shop (where a front line assistant was told by her supervisor 'you'll never get rid of the queue if you do that for every customer' upon seeing her offer a couple of options to a grateful customer) just reassuring him or herself that there's no chance of anyone impressing the customer tonight.

Later that evening my friend John and I sit, stomachs rumbling, at a table amongst the smokers at a pizza restaurant. It being so busy, we couldn't be accommodated elsewhere.

It's heaving, but service is ticking along, and we enjoy our dough balls (we're consenting adults). My head starts to spin round, as is my wont when I perceive that people who have entered after us are receiving their main courses ahead of us. Feeling bewildered at the lack of natural justice, we call over the waitress and ask if there's a problem. She removes herself to the ovens to enquire on our behalf but delays her return.

After a further twenty minutes she returns again, believing we've finished. We explain the main courses have yet to arrive and she again apologises. John stops her and orders a couple of beers. 'To compensate for the poor service,' he explains, 'you could give us the beers on the house.'

She hesitates. Why does she need to hesitate? But she does. 'I'll have to ask,' she says. She does. She returns with the pizzas. 'The beers are on us,' she announces.

She was a very well presented, charming young girl and, to be fair, she may have been a new recruit, but what's with the resistance? Eleven months in and we're back at the start again.

I don't seriously consider withholding my lifetime value from these organisations when they screw up on the service and behave this way, but it narks me considerably. I bet they don't get much time for reflection, I ponder. Another case of no reflection. The Dracula Syndrome is catching.

Several days later I'm discussing service with someone kind enough to pretend to be interested. He's running reception at a large business block in Leeds and we're riffing on service stories. His is a cracker. 'I went into a local supermarket and asked a young assistant standing there: can you point me in the direction of the light-bulbs? After a moment's hesitation, he pointed upwards.'

I hear the response to a recent radio discussion in which I participated. One caller explains that they went to a health store and found there to be only one member of staff present – and she was half way up a step ladder stocktaking. After failing to lurch into frenetic serving action, she's asked by the caller if she's serving. 'Just a moment,' she replies without turning her head. Several moments later, the by now frustrated shopper issues a brusque, 'I'm not here for the good of my health you know,' before realising that, as she was currently in a health store purchasing mixed seeds, she actually was there for the good of her health.

So, November ticks along steadily, frost and rain taking turns to harass my plants. Days out continue to reflect few examples of great service recovery or, equally and even more rarely, unexpected extras.

The typical experience is somehow concentrated into a visit my wife makes to a main post office branch in a local town in 2004. The purpose of the visit is to pay them £5 to check over our son's passport renewal application. To be fair, we'd completed the paperwork several months ago and, like most things, it's been sitting around in the kitchen waiting for us to go and obtain a passport photograph.

So the day arrives and, with expectations of a queue but with a certain rush of reassurance as an after-effect, my wife strides in.

She hands over the envelope containing the documents together with a cheque for £5. 'I'm sorry, where did you get that figure from?' is the first, warm, welcoming response. 'It's £6 for us to check it.'

'That's what it said on the form,' responds my wife.

'Well, these charges changed a long time ago.'

My wife ponders whether to beg forgiveness – 'I'm sorry for leaving it on top of the fridge for so long' – but responds instead, 'Fine. Here's another pound.'

Without looking up, Mrs Misery starts to check the documents. 'You do realise you have to pay the £6 whether you've completed them rightly or wrongly, don't you?'

'Yes,' responds my wife, at the same time feeling herself sliding into the depressive caverns of the levels of frustration I experience.

I think it is at this point that the concept of armed customers might provoke a different reaction but, joking apart, the whole ordeal – and it is an ordeal – just makes you want to leave for some fresh air, to drive away the smell of gloomy indifference.

If the post office is going to sell an increased range of other products and services, they do indeed have a great neighbourhood hook to build upon. However, their traditional values of reliability and service will soon be compromised if this experience is being reproduced across the country.

By November, we've started to laugh at some of these

experiences. While broadly underwhelming, they often raise a snigger, such is the lack of understanding, perspective and ownership amongst the people we meet.

So here we are, encircling the cheese counter at a Tyneside department store, having decided to make off with some Northumbrian cheese. Ahead of us is a young man who is in mid-conversation with one of the two boys serving. We anticipate something akin to our Brighouse experience: professional and effortless patronage, courtesy, warm interaction and fulfilment. Am I asking for too much? I'm afraid the next customer is, as you're about to discover.

'I'd like to try that one,' he points to one of the cheeses. The assistant takes a small knife and removes a piece so thin and translucent that you could use it as a contact lens or a spare fingernail. If you dine at his house, I bet he serves *petits threes*.

'Em … OK,' stumbles the customer and the cheese is proffered towards him.

'I, er, can't taste it. Can I have a bigger piece, please?'

'No.'

NO? I can't believe this. Surely any cheesemonger worth his salt (or saltman worth his cheese) would know that we Brits, having tasted, feel obliged, through a deep-seated tendency towards honour, to complete the purchase.

Is there a fundamental lack of perspective here? Cheesemongers of the sort encountered here are used to a certain type of clientele who regard cheese with the same passion as fine wines, football or even religion.

He genuinely hasn't received enough cheese to detect any taste at all. Looking slightly bewildered and bracing himself for an apology, he waits, eyebrows raised for a recovery. It doesn't come. He still picks a small, pre-wrapped piece and wanders towards the tills.

A few embarrassing moments pass and we, having learned from the experience, simply indicate the cheese we want and leave.

It's the sort of thing that happens at many shops I visit.

I regularly go in and try to assess, from the activity within, what managers have set out as key business priorities.

My conclusion from what's happened this year is as follows:

Inconvenience Stores: Performance Priorities

1 Stocktaking (always up a ladder or behind the bread shelf)
2 Rearranging sandwiches so that the least fresh are at the front
3 Never having any books of stamps, in spite of openly advertising their availability
4 Telling people the car wash / passport photo machine / toilet is out of order (and posting a note saying 'engineer aware')
5 Broadcasting to all and sundry the fact that a credit card transaction has been refused by the customer's bank
6 Sundry activities
7 Overt, irresponsible sales practices
8 Customer Service

If this isn't the case, then the one local shop where I regularly ask for stamps but never have them (and should) would respond to my next enquiry with, 'I'm sorry about this. I've had a word to make sure we get a bigger stock in.' But it doesn't happen.

Then it's off to a reunion with some old mates. We stay at a South Yorkshire hotel. It's one that, many years ago, when I was a student in the area, used to be frequented by the rich and famous. Clearly, the gentrification of the surrounding area had gone ahead without it, as it has clearly seen better days. But, significantly, on a reunion weekend, the quality of the hotel décor is less important a worry than your receding hairline and expanding girth and your erstwhile classmates' response.

One is expecting to be very thirsty and possibly to overdo the drink, so, again, the hotel is just there as a beacon at the crash landing site.

In such cases, even the breakfast does not rush up the

'rated as important by customers' chart, as it simply fulfils a biological need to restore energy, sugar and salt levels so that the body can be dragged to a newsagents.

But what is important – and I gather most hoteliers are aware of this – is checking in and checking out. Smooth, personal, effective and, most of all, quick. The experience of the former is fine. The place is empty, and all requirements are fulfilled, with some humour to boot.

However, upon departing on the Sunday, I think I've spotted a flaw in the plan. First of all, given that there were several hen parties staying at the hotel, people generally arrive as late as possible for Sunday breakfast.

So I part my eyelids with a shoehorn and walk downstairs. On greeting the breakfast waitress, I discover that my voice, through leading my colleagues in some impromptu community singing the evening before, has dropped several octaves and, to quote a recent review of a Tom Waits recording, sounds like I'm 'trying to regurgitate a particularly hairy pork scratching'.

I am quite early. It's deserted and it's 9.30. Only an hour to go before breakfast ends. So, not unnaturally, a good three dozen guests emerge from 10.00 onwards, leading to bottlenecks at the grapefruit juice and a run on fried eggs.

The team, once leaning around and smiling, now ferret around. But, by and large, they manage the service effectively. 'I bet they're used to this sort of ebb and flow,' says yours truly, and truly profoundly.

The attempt to check out some minutes later reveals how wrong I am. My man at reception is alone and there are eight people in the queue to check out. He sticks religiously to his process of confirming bills, printing invoices, drawing the credit card through the reader and issuing a correctly folded receipt.

The process appears unnecessarily laborious and he appears to take an unnatural joy in ensuring each interaction equals the previous in terms of time taken (to the second) and language used.

He smiles at each guest and bids them farewell, but the people in the queue behind me quite rightly point out that the hotel might expect there to be a few people checking out in the half-hour after breakfast. The moon is generally more populated than this reception desk.

There's a reassuring circularity in the fact that his religious efficiency is neatly reflected by a gospel choir, in a nearby suite, chorusing praise and giving thanks.

My man is not to blame. He, in fact, is producing all of the 'human' elements we've singled out as significant. The hotel's handling of the 'basics', however, is wanting and the sight of a colleague running to assist would have been like manna from the heaven being invoked by those rousing voices.

November spawned a monster, once sang Morrissey. I wouldn't go so far as to describe this month as being horrifying, but the incredible inconsistency and lack of joined-up service sends a shiver down the spine.

12

December

'And, in the end, the love you take is equal to the love you make.'
Lennon/McCartney 1969

I've set out to offer up an unbiased, fair perspective on UK customer service levels. When it's been execrable, I have resisted identifying the culprits in the perhaps misguided hope that as well as these organisations recognising themselves, others will use the stories to road-test their service and to encourage discussion and improvement.

After all, how do we know this wouldn't happen in our organisation? We probably don't, so we should make some attempt to find out.

Where I've found great service – great 'out of the ordinary' extras or fantastic service recovery – I've provided more description, so some of you can experience it too. However, the thing is, I can't guarantee the consistency and refund the purchase price of this book if you discover Prêt's weakest link, for example, or promise you a 30% discount even if you aren't really a teacher. But it would be nice for people to recognise themselves and their own organisations and the good that they do.

Service is anchored in the human psyche and all of the idiosyncrasies of our everyday behaviour. As such, I've tried to de-mystify the complexities of service design and focus on the part that makes the greatest contribution.

I've explained how important it is that people on the 'front line' understand the business context. I've presented the importance of the increased levels of ownership that ensue. I've baulked at the barriers erected to frustrate us and celebrated the sense of liberty that characterises those organisations who have placed their own people and customers at the heart of their business, not just in adverts or on posters, but in the day-to-day activities their job descriptions tell them to do.

I've also set us consumers a challenge. Two identical interactions may look the same, smell the same and require the same output. Logical thinking makes you believe that's the case, but the human factor always means there's a chance of a rogue element interfering.

So let's be fair to our frontline employees in this country. They can only go so far towards defusing our frustrations and emotions. Once we overstep the mark and start to treat them unfairly (and we do it damned unpleasantly at times) we erode their confidence, their belief in being customer-focused, which in turn reduces the percentage of great service moments.

Thus begins the swirling vicious circle, the never-ending descent into more monologue exchanges, indifference and dismay.

So, to paraphrase Lennon and McCartney, you've got to make the effort.

Particularly apposite is a recent experience, way beyond the time-frame of this book. But so fresh in the memory that I fume still.

Having recently bought a PC, I receive a letter from the Group office of the retailer explaining to me that the credit agreement I had signed for a percentage of the cost had not been forwarded by the store to their finance company. Could I therefore choose from the following list of options (including re-visiting the store to complete the form again, sending in a copy of the original, making the payment by alternative means) and let them know what I plan to do?

I am away at the time, so a week or so passes before I deal with the correspondence. Practising what I preach, I decide to telephone and apologise for not returning it. I do. I speak to a friendly woman who says that she'll note the conversation. 'It'll be a week before I can get into the store,' is the last thing I say.

A few days later I receive a second letter from the author of the first. On this occasion the tone is darker and, while I'm not threatened with imprisonment, there is a barely concealed threat that 'further action may be taken'. And isn't it funny that when you want organisations to take action they don't? But when they need you, they take action.

I check the DDI at the foot of the page and ring immediately to explain my anger. The phone rings and rings. No voicemail message, no divert, no person explaining options or a return to the main switchboard (often a description preferred to anything indicating the presence of a human).

I leave it ten minutes and sit slowly casseroling on my seat. Two further attempts prove fruitless, so I opt for the main office number at the top of the page. On this occasion I encounter an automated number-selection process which has more layers than Garfield's favourite lasagne. Even choosing 'to make a complaint' produces four options, none of which is 'to make a complaint'.

As my anger builds like bile rising in a queasy stomach, I eventually get through to a young man who sounds like he has been disturbed from his mid-morning nap by my call.

He immediately and unwisely attempts to use humour to defuse the situation, which even I, the most even-tempered person in the universe, regard as further intimidation.

I explain my anger at the fact that my telephone call hasn't been recorded. I explain the fact that the letter is unnecessary and bordering on the aggressive. I explain that all I want is to be able to have a discussion, raise my concerns, but ultimately confirm that I'm going to send in the original agreement. He promises to take the details and follow it up for me. The follow-up? To this day … you can guess the rest.

His attempts to connect me fail so I hang up and try the original DDI line again. On this occasion the third attempt produces a result. A woman answers, introduces herself and explains that the person I'm attempting to call is on holiday.

I explain, with some justification, all the ways they could instantly improve their business performance. I resist sarcasm, which would have been understandable in these circumstances, and listen as she explains that these second letters are automatically generated several days after the first letter if a reply has not been received, irrespective of a call from the customer, as it happens.

She accepts the rigidity of the system may lose them customers, even though they are only related to the retailer selling the original PC by their belonging to the same Group. She explains that they've raised the issue with management and that other customers are equally frustrated. And when I think about it, I recall that her response to my call was to ask immediately: 'Is it about a letter you've received?'

I, for the first time in a long while, complete the conversation, put down the phone and chuck a wheelbarrow-load of expletives about the place, like a particularly cross Ozzy Osbourne.

When I finally calm down, I put my thoughts in writing, as she has suggested. I try to be as helpful as possible, in a seething, serial-killer kind of way, not quite resisting the urge to describe their service as about 'as useful as a chocolate fireguard'. But I address it to the manager whose name appears at the foot of both letters.

Several days later, the efforts of the guy in complaints appear not to have borne any fruit, as he has yet to come back to me. The reply to my letter will, probably, take even longer. But while it's out there in their hands, there's always the chance that someone, somewhere will start to put two and two together, realise the power of great recovery and give me a ring.

I sense that there are few channels for internal feedback in this organisation. Few opportunities for employees to 'get things off their chests'. Few chances to criticise constructively where it makes sense – and no apparent recognition or reward for doing so.

My feelings are of guilt and shame. Why did I choose this

retailer? Even though they were pretty good by and large (see earlier) I feel foolish now. I'm not expecting the retailer to warn off future customers by telling them that if anything goes awry, their lives will be made a misery. But having told a couple of friends about the purchase, I feel the need to remain tight-lipped on the matter of the after-sales, in case they remember the conversation and recklessly recommend the organisation to someone else.

A friend has a similar experience with a really good Internet grocery-shopping organisation, which she recommends unreservedly to anyone who enquires. Her experience was the one where the organisation knows that there is a problem but avoids honesty in favour of promising that 'it might be a little late'.

After the combination of indifference, rudeness, failure and unfulfilled promises that ensues, it all ends with the admission that they've grown faster than anticipated and are struggling to maintain the service. Her first instinct is to ring her friends and apologise.

I hear about the French couple who were being sued by relatives of the victim of a crash caused by a drunk driver. They had invited the perpetrator to a dinner party and were being accused of not having taken sufficient precautions to prevent the accused from driving home. It won't be long before someone charges me with aggravated recommendation of a PC retailer.

It won't have escaped your attention throughout this book that I spend a lot of time with people talking about service. I also get to see the inner workings of organisations that have our best interests at heart because they know they serve their own. So what advice do I have for organisations engaged in producing a return for their customers, reward for their stakeholders and respect for the greater community?

First of all, service is a complicated thing to deliver perfectly. There are a number of reasons for this. The prevailing context in recent years is unhelpful. Whether it's a returning tremor from the self-focused 80s or a misguided interpretation of liberty as 'consumers rule', society is clearly more self-ish than it used to be and may, as the Iron Lady once affirmed, have been completely extinguished in favour of rampant individualism.

Whatever the combination of factors at play, this has produced infinitely more testing customers with, as often as not, a higher opinion of their standing than is actually merited. The next time I hear the statement 'do you know who I am?' I am prepared to share the list of Anglo-Saxon adjectives and nouns I have prepared specifically for the opportunity.

I see this in the frankly nasty broadsides fired at frontline personnel around the country, from the delightful team at WH Smith in King's Cross Station to ticket-sellers at Highbury Stadium. It's not their fault you missed your train, or that you didn't get in touch soon enough to reserve a seat. It's not a question of fault; it's a question of our society's values – our community's tenets and principles. Ours, in the UK, seem to exhibit selfism over philanthropy, enclosure over openness and predictability over the risk associated with going out on a limb for a fellow man.

Which takes me to the challenge of instilling your values into your business. Too many of the organisations I encountered are 'plain' - not even bordering on the sweetness of vanilla - simply manilla envelopes of increasing tedium. It's rare that I encounter an experience that implies some decent higher purpose, be it interest in the customer, the community or some highly regarded precept or belief.

If your main value is honesty, then any complaint should be met with an honest response, delivered in a process that generates impressions of honesty, that rewards it when it happens amongst staff, that targets it through its performance management systems.

If you proudly boast that people are your greatest resource and you nod sagely at every conference speaker who mentions the link between happy employees and happy customers, then why is it only fast-track people who get rich personal development support? Why are training sessions and personal development updates, coaching sessions and staff briefings postponed at the first sign of an 'operational' crisis? Why does no-one get thanked for a piece of work well done and why can you count the number of recognition awards you've made on one hand when you have thousands of employees?

I am not suggesting mass 'tree-hugging' exercises and I do not own shares in an outward-bound management-training centre. Values are tangible and should be synonymous with the organisation's brand, if brand is appropriate.

Values can come easily. Football clubs simply look at the motto on their club crest and they spring out, albeit in Latin. However, it's ensuring that employees can draw upon them for guidance when handling difficult situations. This only works where managers in the business, all those people with responsibility for others, are seen to live by them day in day out.

In large organisations in particular, this is only usually effective when they are actively encouraged, i.e. paid, to do so. And what should they be paid to do? How about spending time giving feedback to the front line? How about asking the front line how they feel about particular business issues? How about eliciting ideas and hunches from them, rather than presenting the issue and imposing your own solution, however well meant?

I've come across several pieces of research in my time equating employee involvement, in these ways, with engagement, responsibility, flexibility and ownership. Ownership again – that common requirement of all customers. It goes without saying that it improves productivity. But it doesn't happen much during my year of discovery.

Large organisations, from my experiences of dealing with their frontline employees, appear to engage them in change through a combination of financial reward and thinly disguised bullying, in the form of direct imposition of managers' will. It's good to introduce an important issue and invite discussion. It's not good to greet ideas with a warm nod and then acquiesce with the devil by simply introducing a response that the management team has dreamed up prior to the meeting.

If sales are the desired output of effort, then let's target sales. Let's forget about the process used to generate the figures, and focus on the figures themselves. That appears to be the approach.

Do that and you end up with the situation in many retail banks today. You pre-qualify for this credit card, you could get this loan, why not try our mortgage? No attempt to uncover a real need for the service, just another credit card lead, just another opportunity to generate a personal loan … and don't forget to sell the personal loan insurance in case they can't afford to pay.

Many retail banking employees I speak to genuinely dislike this approach, but when it means you can take home a 20% bonus at the end of the year, you fall into line. Oh, and the fact it's the only element of performance contributing to your boss's pay rise tends to focus his or her interventions too.

Here, we make the conditions for service to thrive, even more difficult. Staff who are bonused according to sales are not sufficiently focused on the customers' needs, but on their own. Customers feel the warmth of being picked out specially for the new visa card, but find the Marie Celeste where once there lived a customer service/after-sales department. It's not good enough to temper the sales performance by introducing a service-based KPI; it's more deep-seated than that. It requires a fundamental change in the way the organisation is built. It's an intellectual threshold beyond which few have passed.

So, no perspective for frontline people, no reason for managers to provide it and no evidence of it in the majority of transactions I've experienced. And let's stress it again: I am not expecting fantasy service with every transaction. Simply a bit of flair when things go wrong – or a piece of real magic occasionally, perhaps when I least expect it.

Some employees have taken it by the scruff of the neck and, by reason of their personalities, recognise what counts. By asking for feedback and by enveloping every transaction in a warm conversation, they are able to take a regular temperature check of service expectations and introduce them into their repertoire. Hats off to yer man at the Bagel factory again.

It's nice that some organisations, including a major fashion retailer, have changed some processes to try and achieve this. For example, having someone at the front of the store to welcome customers, respond to questions and promote engagement. In reality, however, the people in these roles appear nervous, slow to pick up on real opportunities and a little directionless, as if unsure of the purpose of their role.

Service is complicated because we Brits appear to regard its delivery as the responsibility of the serving classes. We're right back in the old empire and the perfidious Albion is unwilling to declare any semblance of flexibility that may be perceived as tending towards obsequiousness.

Since we appear to link service and servility and cannot find the heart to regard customer service as a profession, its profile is not going to rise above ground level. Cheap labour, taking inbound calls by clockwork, having to ask permission to go to the toilet. That may take you back to some of the worst days of the empire, but it still goes on in many contact centres today.

Customer service training courses have also contributed to the current sorry circumstance. Though well meant and often fantastically well produced and delivered, they exist without context; are led by an outsider, more often than not; are linked neither in practical nor in achievable terms to the higher purpose; and, even where there are a sound set of values in place, they are seen as anything other than a day out for the staff.

Managers occasionally turn up to launch the session, to say how important it is and to stress the importance of change. Then they leave. Some enlightened organisations bring all the people together and create opportunities for people to observe each other and give feedback. Some enlightened organisations challenge their people and ask, 'why bother?' Unless someone can produce a business case for changing the status quo, then we'll close the session now.

The training session closes and even when personal commitments to change are sought, the lack of any apparent management belief and commitment and the failure of the organisation to produce a process to follow up on the training produce indifference. Great enthusiasm and nice feedback scores immediately the workshop has finished, but little evidence that anything has changed six weeks down the road.

Service is complicated because I'm a sales guy and you're a quality man. I'm a person who sets out his life as a series of material steps forward. Tailor-made suit, first BMW, holiday home in the Alps. You're a 9 to 5 guy, family comes first, not tough enough around the edges, not battle-hardened enough. I'm clever enough to design the business so that I get rewarded even if service is rubbish. You soldier on, bathing in the respect of your colleagues, but it's really just a shroud of inconsequence.

Such are the human politics of business. Such is the complexity of internal organisational relationships. A service strategy in a large company belongs to the senior manager sponsoring it, not the people beneath him (usually) or her (more rarely). Its success or failure largely depends on his armoury, his political experience and manoeuvrability. The point is: customer service will prevail if they want it to.

Sure, the consultant tells us to reverse the hierarchy and place customers and staff at the top and the CEO at the bottom. What would this mean? Though well meant, it would mean the CEO deciding life here is too risky and it would be more sensible to go and work somewhere else. It's down to the CEO. Full stop.

Service is complicated because we need the senior manager's support to get some investment in the first place.

These people only like news to be good. Bad news needs to fester around the lower end of the hierarchy.

And when we get the support, we know that reciprocation may require returning a favour for a man called Carmine with friends in Sicily.

Service is complicated because we've built our organisations on a model designed for enacting a process, not for stirring emotion.

Service is complicated because it carries an amateur dramatics-style 'not serious' moniker. Time is taken to carry out interminable reviews but never available for one-to-one coaching sessions, and service improvement discussions have to happen down the Dog and Duck. Like charity circles and fundraising, extra-curricular activities, it's an amateur focus, not really part of what we do here.

However, my experiences appear to have highlighted a few organisations, where subsequent research has identified a unifying thread.

A Chief Executive or senior management team who believe in the power of differentiation through service. People brave enough to regard 'personal development' as a leading KPI. If we're up to date, we're doing well. If people see that prioritised in this business, they'll feel better about themselves and, as Happy Computers prove (an organisation where the CEO spends a lot of time sat at reception greeting customers), they'll produce the goods for the organisation – in actual fact and metaphorically.

I have participated in many discussions revolving around establishing a business case for investment in customer service. These are not like conversations prior to investment in product design or marketing campaigns or IT implementation projects. Instincts tell us that the service-based approach is right. However, your average financial accountant needs to see incontrovertible evidence before investment is given. Do we need to change his attitude? Or do we have to change ours?

As I write, in late 2004, it's budget-planning time. That

intriguing procedure where managers propose budgets for next year and take them to the financial people to have them ridiculed. The friend I speak to today tells me that the two things that were questioned in his proposal were the amount to be spent on training (improving the skills of customer-facing people) and the amount to be spent on membership of a cross-sector benchmarking group (helping the organisation develop an external perspective). You have to give the financial guy credit for at least identifying two of the wisest entries in the original budget.

But my friend knows which parts will have been pruned when he receives the gracious approval of his shortsighted peer.

Dilbert, by and large, gets it right. Service is complicated for a number of reasons, but principally because of the human factor. Senior managers in organisations have generally arrived at their positions through a combination of technical knowledge and political experience and expediency.

'You're with the sharks now,' a colleague told me when I arrived at a middle-ranking management position several years ago. Now, I'm not asking for a world where every new management appointee is told, 'you're with the teddy bears now and they really need a cuddle,' but it does highlight the lack of organisational focus behind the great tragedy of poor UK service. What we get is a true representation of the personality of most of the businesses in the UK.

These personalities do unconsciously guide the behaviours of the people in their sway. Frontline employees look to the furthest management point and interpret direction from the words and actions of these individuals. As often as not the words are uniformly positive, vibrant, forward-looking and encouraging. But it's the actions that are most telling, and the failure of the latter to match the former in many UK organisations lies at the root of the problem.

'People are our greatest asset,' they say, but no people-related key performance indicators appear anywhere on their business scorecards. 'Customer comes first,' they cry, but they stop short of further investigation when it begins to emerge that really listening to the customer would imply making significant differences to the way we work.

There is the story of the family diner chain for whom chicken wings are a popular starter. The newly-appointed marketing director, apparently on a whim, decides to replace them as a starter with chicken satay.

Around the country diners are settling in to their chairs, perusing the menu and confirming the choice of chicken wings as a starter. 'I'm sorry, sir. We don't do them as a starter any more. Would you like to try the satay, sir, it's really good?'

No one wants the satay. Everyone wants the chicken wings. The waitresses, customer-focused to the bitter end, suggest taking a half portion of the main course version of chicken wings and serving that, to meet their customers' requirements. Their colleagues quickly pick up this trick and, within days, this creative response is replicating itself up and down the country, like a quickly replicating sort of thing.

However, as each customer requests the bill, the waitresses have no code under which to key the half portion. 'Use chicken satay,' someone wisely suggests.

Several weeks later, in a distant office, a Marketing Director smiles smugly over his pay packet, hugely enhanced by a fantastic bonus, earned through sales of satay.

So I return to my wanderings about the UK, genuinely hardened by the knowledge that the conditions conspiring to generate the indifferent experiences I record are often far away from the front line, more often than not, talking about the next big car they're about to buy.

There is no code of ethics or core values at play in the vast majority of my experiences. People have neither the perspective nor the attitude to take me down a fantasy tangent, where my specific, individual need is remarkably met. People are genuinely in fear of the customer and have had the spark frightened out of them like a ferreted rabbit.

People earn £4.90 an hour. That's a possible cause.

•

It's a sunny day in Cambridgeshire as two friends decide to have a day out with their four children. As one of the children suffers from cerebral palsy and is currently confined to a wheelchair, every journey is usually made by car. On this occasion, to the delight of the children, they're going into town on the bus.

Having carefully checked the timetable from their village to the town, our family group makes its way slowly to the bus stop, where the kids excitedly examine the schedule and make plans for the rest of the day. It's 11.30 in the morning when the bus pulls up. It does not have the low threshold enabling wheelchair-bound customers to mount with ease. It is also a single driver bus.

Dismayed, the mother of the four-year-old disabled child struggles with the wheelchair, as her friend attempts to hold the disabled child, his 16-month-old sibling and keep an eye on her own two children. The mother looks up to the driver who is watching in silence.

'Can't you help me?' she asks, clearly distressed by the struggle.

'No, I can't help you.' His exact words. They find a place from which to echo within the woman's subconscious, so cold and unhelpful. The driver is subject to rules which restrict the time he can be absent from his cabin. This the girls discover later. At no time are they told this during the experience. The driver is also subject to health and safety constraints which limit the heavy lifting he can do during the day. This the girls discover later.

Astonished, the mother of the disabled child looks down the half-full bus, hoping to catch the eye of a sympathetic fellow traveller. Most of the occupants of the bus are mature or elderly people. Most stare, some look away or downwards at their newspapers.

By now the bus has been stationary for some time. All of the children are becoming distressed, as the mother finally gets the wheelchair onto the bus, with the help of a solitary young Indian lady who emerges from among the passengers and makes a valiant attempt to help the family group get settled into their seats.

'It can't be easy for you,' observes an elderly lady to the mother, as she finally rests back into her seat. The mother, visibly upset by the whole experience, resists the temptation to say what she really thinks.

Once in town, what had been planned as a great pioneering day out, has turned out to be a miserable scuttle around, searching for options for the homeward journey.

Only the buses from the immediate suburbs have the wheelchair threshold fitted, so, defeated but stronger for the experience, the group pays £25 to find an adequately-sized taxi to take them the five miles home.

The email sent to the customer feedback page on the travel company website remains unanswered some three months after the event.

•

Of all the things that cause customers to stay loyal, buy more and recommend to friends and family, it's the quality of the experience that really matters. Within the customer experience, it's the human factor – ownership – above products, prices and processes, that really matters, and without a truly engaged employee, valued, involved, respected and engaged, nothing will change.

There are those meriting praise, though. There are those who, through their own stubbornness, belief in the power of the human spirit or pure selfishness based on the premise that good service makes money, will carry the standard into battle. There are those who pick up the standard from colleagues who are forced down through internal politics. There are those with a capacity for creativity and for understanding how organisations should be designed, who deserve our credit.

The relentlessly cheerful supervisor at Harry Ramsden's in Guiseley, who sees a bunch of kids as an opportunity, not a problem.

Wendy, at Air Miles, whose dual life includes running an

excellent contact centre and singing in an Abba tribute band, and who has deservedly won awards for her passion.

Sam at Pizza Hut, for knowing exactly what a young family want from a visit to the restaurant and for having that rare combination of values, attitude and skills to deliver it, consistently, day in day out.

Gearoid at the Bagel Factory, for recognising that customers are people and a smile is a disappearing species in this country.

The team at Brown Sugar in Durham, for making a family feel welcome and adding a new 'must do' to the tourist list in Durham (cathedral, castle and Brown Sugar).

Leopard-skin-shoe lady at Loch Fyne in Harrogate, for making us feel really important and for, again, seeing kids as an opportunity rather than an obstacle.

John and the team at Czerwik for the great traditions of good service, the right balance of formality with improvisation, great technical knowledge and an ability to generate passion in all but the most cold-hearted visitor.

The team at WH Smith at King's Cross who, in the face of regular misery, produce reliability, speed and good humour. I wish their employers a speedy recovery!

The ticket inspector at GNER who keeps us amused with his sotto voce observations.

The assistant on the Virgin Train into Edinburgh, who considers it just as important to use humour to connect with his customers as it is to connect with the right platform.

The girl who took me around Borders in Chicago so that I could find everything I was looking for, and her colleague, who applied a price reduction even though I wasn't really a teacher. For their creativity, flexibility and downright friendliness, raise your glasses.

For the fish and chip lady on the road back to Oban, and for the volunteer at the seal watch in Inverness.

For Alison Widdup, for having the courage to recognise the limitations of our conventional thinking on contact centres, and for having the talent to do something about it.

For Vern the Butcher and part-time calendar boy, his humour, warmth and knowledge of his craft. His unstinting focus on his people. His customers are his friends, but they are well-off too, having discovered that the best produce is sourced locally and that supermarkets are unable to give your family direct advice on what they're eating.

For Richard the fishmonger – up at all hours and able to produce a meticulous, metronomic preparation style, as great to watch as to enjoy the fruits of his work.

For Lee, Ian and the team at Coffee Culture, for providing a haven for all who share this frustrating passion for people, this labour of love: trying to make businesses understand that service only flourishes where its people flourish too.

They almost bring a question mark into my book's title: inconvenience stores? But they are still in the minority in the UK today. My year in UK customer service has found little evidence of the magic formula and many examples of the obstacles that remain still.

Most of us play the dual role here. Most of us are customers and employees. Most of us decry the lack of courtesy and ownership I've encountered but wander sheep-like, in a dream state, through the very same organisations that produce the grey indifference of service in this country today. We know what's wrong but someone else can do something about it.

So, when the CEO is stirred from his early-evening aperitif by the unwelcome external call and we once again stand by as the ticket-seller is abused, I tot up the points, put down my pen and assess the balance of my year.

I think, perhaps, that we might just get the service we deserve.

Thanks

Thank you, reader. I hope it's been worth it. If you agree and you want to help me raise the profile of service, then email your stories, good and bad, to my publisher's website: **admin@ardrapress.com**.

I want especially to thank John Hughes, Jackie Matthews and the rest of our team at Customer Service Network (CSN). John has been a great source of ideas and inspiration. He too carries the scars of poor service experiences and has the unhappy knack of appearing to generate appalling service wherever he goes (especially on trains). Recently described by a new acquaintance as 'Mr Exceeding Expectations' due to his passion and achievements, he's braver than I am at pointing out service discrepancies, and has almost sparked off a number of customer uprisings in many West Midlands-based high street outlets.

At CSN, our network of organisations, aiming for differentiation through the quality of service, has given us many insights into what the truly positive organisations are doing. The experience has also taught me that we're only as strong as our weakest link. That's why I've not identified the organisations providing the less impressive customer experiences. The fact is: it could happen to anyone. How strong is *your* weakest link?

Our business believes in the power of learning, and if this book leads your team to start collecting more data on your own organisation's performance, then it will have been worth the effort.

Customer Service Network helps organisations improve their business performance through networking, education and research. Check it all out at **www.customernet.com**.

A special thank you to Tony Locke at Unisys. Tony is the man behind the Unisys/Management Today Service Excellence Awards, and he gave me the opportunity to participate in the process as an assessor several years ago. His continuing kindness, support and good humour (in spite of supporting Villa) have been one of many candles in the darkest days of this service travelogue.

If your organisation wants to prove that it is really delivering service excellence, I would recommend a visit to **www.serviceexcellenceawards.com** where you can take the ultimate test.

There are many other people who have sat stony-faced over the last two years as I've recounted my experiences and who have promised to buy this book, if only to make me go away. Thanks to them and, er, chequebooks out, boys.

The big 'thank you' (and tell them what they've won, Dave!) goes to:

Lee, Ian and co at Coffee Culture, for putting up with the same stories repeated thousands of times, and humouring me with a knowing smile each time I tentatively offered up a release date for the book.

Joan Roca for taking service into the stratosphere and for providing the ultimate benchmark.

Jon Fitzmaurice for presiding over my 18 months at a homelessness campaigning charity ten years ago and for demonstrating just how far you can go with the right values and beliefs. And again, Jon, thanks for inserting into a strategic document my contribution to the organisation's mission statement in 1993 ('to boldly go wherever we can afford').

David King, for supervising my inexorable rise from rank obscurity to semi-obscurity in my previous employ, and for providing the most reliable sounding board an untidy thinker could ever need, as well as an even more reliable smorgasbord whenever we enjoy his hospitality.

David Brooke, for maintaining a watchful eye on service in Kirklees and Calderdale and for those therapeutic lattes.

To Mike Umphray and family, for faith in people and in the future. Good luck, mate, and thanks for all the support.

To Adrian Chiles, a big 'baggie' thank-you for stepping in to write the foreword for the book. Hopefully see you back at the Stadium of Light soon. Not sure in which division, though.

Mark Newman, still the 'best man' – who better to share a radio with on a Saturday afternoon.

Jim Sherwood, for the knock-downs and the 'offal magic' of 82-83.

Xander Leijnse, whose increasing influence towards the end of the journey led to an unfeasibly large number of visits to fine dining establishments and record stores. To Xander, again thanks for helping my children understand that Dutch is really English with a Dutch accent.

Andy Baker, for helping me create an in-house video for a previous employer in which football coaching was used as a metaphor for personal development. The extravagantly care-free humour injected by Andy and consequently contained therein upset so many directors, the video was never used and has now, we like to think at least, entered the realms of the cult. Raise your sunglasses, Andy.

To Alison Widdup, for following her instincts and awakening us all to a new vision of the contact centre. Here's someone who's built a business around some of the beliefs this weary traveller holds close to his heart. After all, isn't it better for everyone? So check out **www.betterforeveryone.com**. Thanks for blazing the trail and for making it easier for the rest of us.

To Colin Marvell, for friendship and for commitment to the belief that humanity wins out in the end. Those who know Colin have come to regard as defunct the adjective 'churchillian'. We all agree that 'marvellian' has the edge when it comes to stoicism, passion and commitment.

James Eagle, for his encouragement, humour and hospitality and for inviting my son and me along to Carrow Road and forgetting that being the perfect host doesn't mean scraping a 1-0 win completely against the run of play (and no way should Oster have been sent off).

To Kevin Smith for the Celtic shirt anecdote and emotional Football Aid memories.

To Neil Baldwin for guidance, insight and belief (he follows Palace).

To Rick Lent, a great service-excellence hero who, many years ago, happened upon our little team in a large retail banking organisation. Rick articulated the challenges of service excellence with such blinding clarity that even I started to feel that even I could make a contribution.

To David Jackson for some inspirational input over the years and for many insightful pieces of thought that have been borne out by my experience. I have tried to reflect David's passion and expertise throughout.

To Mark Mellon and family for insights on tourism in West Yorkshire, dodgy tee shirts, that 'I've just flown in from Newcastle and, goodness, my arms are tired' line (never fails), and for hospitality so warm that, on one occasion, I failed to notice I'd fallen into his fireplace.

Andrew Walker ('Carpet Man') for revealing the true habits of dust mites.

To David Gott and the team at St Joseph's RC School, Brighouse, for showing that a genuinely values-led approach can work equally well and with such profoundly affecting results in our education system as in these retail establishments I describe.

There are many more people whose anecdotes, encouragement and support have prodded me along, but none of this would have been possible without the friendship and encouragement of Ronan Fitzsimons, publishing director at Ardra Press. Ronan's a rare combination of wit, grace and technique – the original, real 'one-off'. There will always be a welcoming table set for Ronan and Shell.

To Sunderland AFC for being a lantern in the dark (albeit occasionally leading me down a pit-shaft) and to Louise, Lesley and Mandy and a return to the Promised Land.

To my friends at the FA Premier League, especially Cathy, Kathryn, Sarah and Jo.

To the humour of Bill Hicks, Stewart Francis and Reginald D Hunter (among many others) for providing just the right turn of phrase to inspire my description of any number of unfortunate interactions.

To my Mum and Dad, Kathleen and Michael (Frank & Sean). For being good people, often too good for these times.

To my sister Catherine, for drawing my attention to the additional obstacles faced by disabled customers (my nephew Jack is heroically overcoming cerebral palsy) and to my sister Sarah, for developing the international hand signal for 'beef sandwich' and for pointing out that it's not generally courteous to turn up at relatives' houses and bring your own CDs in. Love to Martin and Tom too, for being too nice to point this out!

To Dylan MJ and Ruby Eve, the next generation of service detectives.

To my Dad, Michael, a thank you in advance for all of the marketing of this book you'll be doing at Annfield Plain Cricket Club. A sales rep for many years, all your relationships were based on warmth, humour and ownership. Now, that rings a bell …

Finally, to my wife Ana and our kids Luis and Elena, who, in spite of the obvious temptation to abandon me at the till, have, like good soldiers, stood and shared the burden.

'Sometimes when I'm speaking to an audience I don't know what to do with my hands,' I once mused. 'Put them over your mouth,' Ana replied.